APACHERIA GOLD
IN THE LAND OF ADAMS

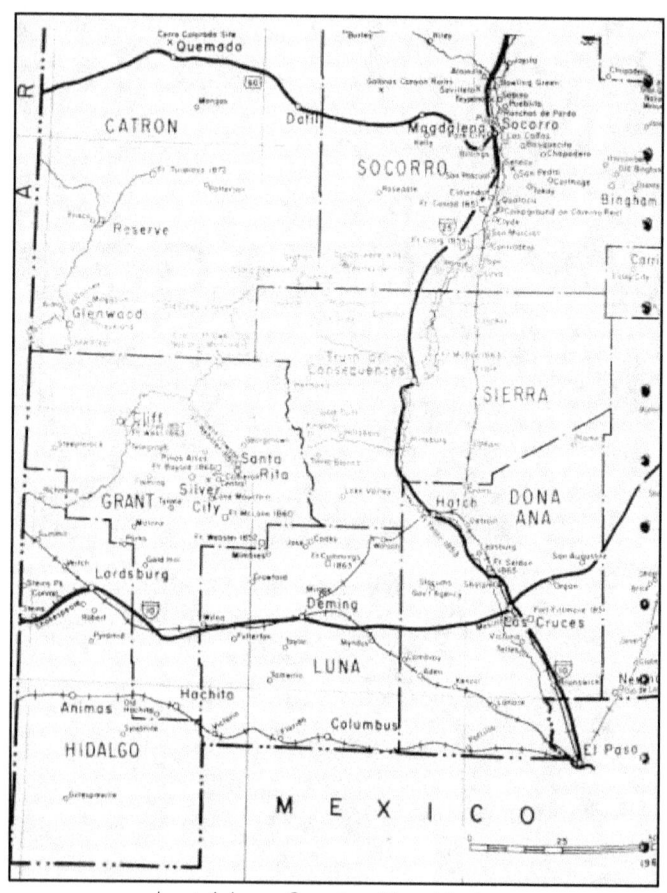

Lost Adams Country, New Mexico.

APACHERIA GOLD
IN THE LAND OF ADAMS

John LeMay

DEAD HORSE HISTORY

A SUBSIDIARY OF BICEP BOOKS. ROSWELL, NEW MEXICO

Printed in the United States of America

LeMay, John.
Apacheria Gold: In the Land of Adams
ISBN 978-1-953221-16-2
New Mexico/Arizona—Treasure/Folklore

For J. Frank Dobie,
I'd like to think you'd have enjoyed it

Lost Adams Mine Found at Last.

Mr. Ed. Owens informs the reporter of the Argus of the discovery of the long lost Adams mine. It all came through John Daisy, an old Indian whom Mr. Owens had befriended in time of need on several different occasions. One day not long ago Mr. Daisy concluded he would return the compliments of Mr. Owens, so he took him over to where the old mine was, and there before them in it's quietness and solitude, with wealth projecting from every nook and crake lay the old mine which has been laying idle for nearly thirty long years. Mr. Owens and associates located several claims, and say they feel confident there will be a big mining boom on before long, as excitement is running high

Every so often, little blurbs like this one, from the *Holbrook Argus* of August 18, 1906, would appear claiming to have found the Lost Adams. Notice the article doesn't say where the strike occurred…

A NOTE FROM THE AUTHOR

"The exact location of the [gold strike] has not yet been announced, and the parties interested decline to give out any of the particulars for publication until all these arrangements have been perfected. It is claimed, however, that it is the old Adams diggings, which were lost many years ago."— Bisbee Daily Review, *August 11, 1904*

S ome authors have the problem of starting a project and never finishing it. I have the problem of starting a book, then letting it balloon into two separate books entirely. It happened with *Tall Tales & Half Truths of Billy the Kid*, where I kept coming across great stories about Pat Garrett. I kicked around the idea of a book on the Kid's killer, and not long after, *Tall Tales & Half Truths of Pat Garrett* was born.

Similarly, in doing *Legend & Lore of the Lost Adams*, I kept coming across some really neat, related treasure stories. Plus I had also promised myself that I would limit this new series of books to a little under 200 pages. Before I knew it, *Legend & Lore of the Lost Adams* had ballooned to nearly 300 pages. And, once again, it seemed logical to re-organize the existing book into two separate tomes. In dividing *Legend & Lore of the Lost Adams*, I decided to remove the more anecdotal accounts and let them encompass their own volume of treasure tales from the "land of Adams" and, thus, a brand-new book was born. Basically, *Apacheria Gold in the Land of Adams* covers gold strikes in the same general area as the diggings, just sans the diggings themselves. The stories included herein are by no means leftovers, either. I would say they are probably of more interest to Lost Adams hunters than those in the first book because they are lesser known and possibly more accurate.

So, with that said, grab your figurative pic-axes and prepare to embark on another armchair journey into the land of Adams…

John LeMay

HUNT FOR GOLD.

Twe Men Get Directions From Convict Where to Find Fabulous Riches.

Lon Jenkins, of Socorro, an old-time miner, and Barney Scertacini, also a mining man, have left Socorro for southwestern New Mexico to hunt the famous Adams diggings. The location of this bonanza was known to but one man, who was serving a term in the penitentiary at Santa Fe. The parents of this man were friends of the parents of Lon Jenkins, in the state of Alabama. These sent the prisoner papers, books, delicacies occasionally, in gratitude for which he sent Lon Jenkins a map and full description of the Adams diggings. Owing to the fact that so many had searched for these diggings without finding them, Jenkins thought they were legendary, and filed away the map. Three years ago the convict also gave a map to Scertacini, and description as well of the diggings, but he, too, gave no further thought to the matter until last week, when he mentioned accidentally to Jenkins about this map. The two men compared their maps and descriptions, and found they tallied exactly, and they at once fitted out an expedition to find the diggings, and set out with it from Socorro.

Another mysterious blurb on the Adams Diggings from the *Albuquerque Citizen* of May 10, 1902.

TABLE OF CONTENTS

Geronimo and his warriors, c.1886.

INTRODUCTION
LOST ADAMS COUNTRY

Once upon a time in the land of little rain roamed a man known only as Adams. His first name had been lost to the sands of time, much like his missing gold mine. For that was the story he spread in every saloon: lost gold. The tale was basically always the same. Adams and a group of prospectors were led to a hidden canyon of gold called Sno-Ta-Hay by "a half-breed Indian" named Gotch Ear. Notable landmarks along the way included a mountain that resembled a woman and a pair of twin peaks in sight of the diggings. The entrance into Sno-Ta-Hay Canyon had a distinct, Z-shaped pattern to it. Actually, Sno-Ta-Hay Canyon was only a prelude to an even richer find a few miles away according to the guide. But the men found themselves amidst so much gold as it was, they didn't see the need to go any further. The guide left and the men prospected a bonanza totaling near $100,000 in some accounts. All was well until Chief Nana and his Apache warriors came along and massacred everyone but Adams and a lone companion. The duo barely escaped with their lives and wandered through the desert. Eventually, a group of soldiers found the men and escorted them to a military fort. Adams returned to California from whence he came and didn't muster the courage to return to the land of the diggings that bore his name until a full ten years later. That was the basic story of Adams, at least.

Where, when, and who Adams was with often varied. At times, he was one of only five or six prospectors; other times it was over twenty men. Adam's lone companion alternated between being an elderly man named Davidson and another shadowy figure known only as the Dutchman. If Nana didn't play the role of the attacking Indian chief, then Cochise or Geronimo stood in. Most times, Adams had stumbled across the gold towards the end of the Civil War in 1864, while other times he found it prior to the war. Sometimes he found the gold among the malpais or along the Plains of San Agustin. The diggings were even "found" up north in the Navajo country on some occasions. And that was all that really mattered: the location of the gold.

Desert scene from Socorro County, New Mexico.

So many differing versions were given of the terrain and its landmarks, that all anyone could really do was triangulate the basic region of the lost diggings. This triangle extended between two points in New Mexico and one in Arizona, those being from Silver City and Grants in New Mexico to Alpine in Arizona. This triangle is actually so wide that it could contain one of the smaller states within its confines. Furthermore, those confines are sparsely populated to this day. Actually, the area was more densely populated during the Old West. That's because, even though the diggings never played out, the area was rich in gold, which led to gold boomtowns like Kingston, Kelly, Hillsboro, and many others in the Magdalena region of New Mexico. It was also amongst the harshest terrain of the territory, the black, lava-scarred landscape of the malpais being the most treacherous. The rivers were paltry, water was sparse, and rains sometimes provided a double-edged sword in the form of devastating deluges. And, if the landscape didn't kill you, the Apache would. Throughout the 1870s and 1880s, what could be called "Lost Adams Country" was periodically terrorized by Apache raiders like Victorio, Geronimo, Nana, and Cochise. Until 1886, when Geronimo surrendered, settlers lived in mortal dread of the Apache raids. Once, Victorio even captured the mines of the Mogollon.

Actually, many of the region's place names came from men who searched for the diggings, such as Cooney, named for Captain James Cooney. Perhaps more significantly, a regional post office even went by the official name of Adams Diggings, New Mexico. Along those same lines, several towns and villages were arguably born of the Lost Adams legend. In his booklet *The Magdalena (New Mexico) Story*, F. Stanley accurately stated that Magdalena was born of prospectors. As evidence, Stanley quoted at length from an article from the *Santa Fe New Mexican* of May 21, 1880. It related that a prospecting trip under the leadership of a Dr. Sturgeon had stopped in the Magdalena Mountains where they "took up claims." The men soon wrote to the *New Mexican* "in a strain of enthusiastic anticipation of wealth."[1]

Though Stanley didn't know it, the Sturgeon expedition of 1880 was headed by the same fort doctor who had treated Adams when he returned from the canyon. As such, many thought that Dr. Sturgeon was in search of Adams' gold when he came to the Magdalena Mountains. Therefore, per Stanley's version, one could argue that the village of Magdalena itself was inadvertently born of the Adams myth.

During that period, and due to the proliferation of gold in the region, almost any lost placer could be considered the Lost

Adams Diggings. "Back in the 1870s, there were no less than four lost diggings stories connected with that part of the Datil Mountains, what is today known as the Gallinas Mountains," author Richard French noted in his book *Return to the Lost Adams Diggings*.[2]

The celebrated Marionette company is to visit this city on March the ninth under the auspices of the recreational department and will play in the auditorium of the city school. Two performances will be given.

The evening show will feature "The Lost Adams' Diggin's," a romance of the Forty Niner days. The movie stars in miniature, who will take part in this are portrait Marionettes of Clark Gable as the lover, Janet Gaynor as the girl, Ernest Torrence as the Forty Niner, William Powell as the gambler, Tully Marshall as the Desert Rat and Richard Dix as the Indian.

As a testament to its popularity, there was even a marionette show devoted to the Lost Adams in the thirties. (*Monroe News Star*, March 7, 1933.)

And that is the topic of this tome: treasures located within and tangentially related to the legendary Lost Adams Diggings. And unlike the elusive gold of Adams, still unfound to this day, some of the sites to be detailed ahead did indeed yield gold, riches, and death…

Section Notes

[1] Stanley, *Magdalena Story*, p.4.
[2] French, *Return to the Lost Adams Diggings*, Kindle Edition.

A TOWN CALLED ADAMS

THE ADAMS DIGGINGS ON THE MAP

There was a time in New Mexico's past when you could quite literally find the Adams Diggings on the map. Seeing this naturally agitated amateur prospectors, who were unaware that it denoted a place named for the Adams Diggings and not the diggings themselves. To be clear, Adams Diggings was never a town, it was just a post office in a small rural community that eventually took on the name of the legend. The post office operated for fifteen years from 1930 to 1945 and was located about 15 miles northeast of Quemado in Catron County, which many Adams enthusiasts believe the diggings existed within. Richard French noted in *Four Days From Fort Wingate*, "One thing [the post office] was never able to claim was that for which it was named."[1]

One prospector that the place puzzled was Paul A. Hale, who stumbled across it during his hunt for the Lost Adams around the year 1970. In *Return to the Lost Adams Diggings*, he recollected that,

> I … eventually came to a place that once bore the name "Adams Diggings." It had been a small village once that got its name from early-day prospectors who were looking for the same thing I was.[2]

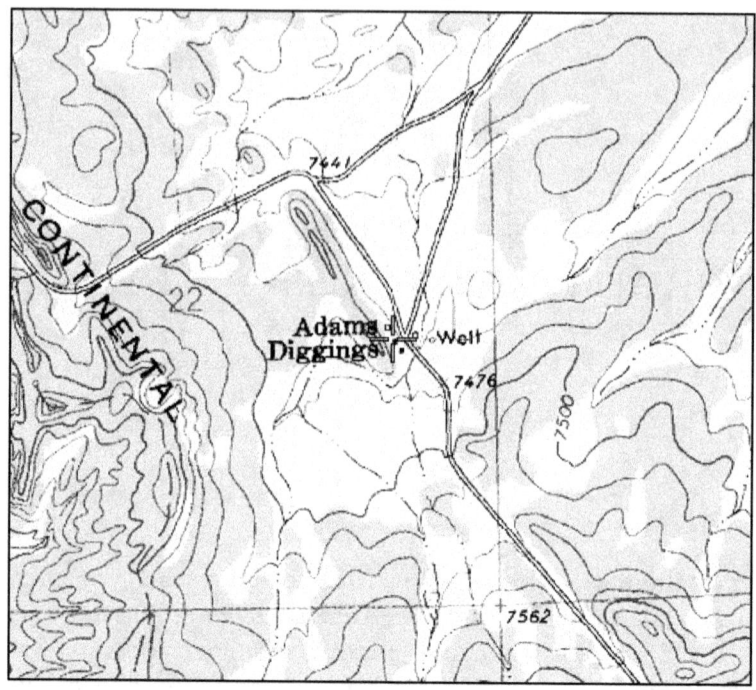

The place also briefly caught the ear of author and explorer David Hatcher Childress, who heard it mentioned during a road trip across New Mexico in the early 2000s. He and a friend had made a pit stop in Reserve, New Mexico when a few of the locals overheard him talking about the Adams Diggings. One of them piped up and told Childress that it was on County Road 603 and was "just the remains of some cabins and fences."[3] The same person also told Childress, "Supposedly, Adams lived up around there. But I don't think he found any gold."[4]

As you can see, apparently a few locals thought the abandoned settlement was the home of Adams himself, which it certainly was not. But how exactly did the place get its name? According to Robert Julyan in *Place Names of New Mexico,* a mischievous NM Highway Department employee put them there. Julyan reported,

As a hobby, an NM Highway Dept. employee had spent time looking for the Diggings, finding only rattlesnakes,

16

and when the employee in 1936 temporarily was assigned to mapmaking, as a joke he put on a draft map a small circle in an uninhabited area N of Pie Town where he'd been searching and labeled it Adams Diggings. Through oversight, the site appeared on the new map and remained there for many years, eliciting numerous inquiries to the Highway Dept.[5]

Shortly after that explanation, Julyan noted the existence of a rural post office in that area "near the site identified on the map." So perhaps we shouldn't say Julyan said that's how the post office got its name, but that's how it got on the map. The Socorro County Historical Society better explained how exactly the post office got its name.

In the late 1990s, area resident Bob Magee revealed that his parents, Guy and Daisy Magee, had named the settlement. They had arrived in the area, about seventeen miles north of Pie Town, in 1916. Back in the late 1920s, Catron County was literally swarming with Adams hunters. The prospectors were likely fired up by articles in the *El Paso Herald* coupled with the great stock market crash of 1929. Prior to this, the Magees had opened a small general store on their ranch. By the 1930s, amateur Adams hunters frequenting the store outnumbered area ranchers. Some of them began asking if they could get their mail forwarded there. Magee eventually obliged and applied to be an official post office. His application was granted in 1930, and when it came time to choose a name, he decided he might as well call it Adams Diggings both as a joke and an enticement. After landing on the map as Adams Diggings, New Mexico, the place was busier than ever. However, Magee said the gold hunters quit coming about the time America entered World War II in the 1940s.

In 1946, the Magees closed their post office, but Adams Diggings remained on the map. If nothing else, it stands as another testament to the legend.

Chapter Notes

---

[1] French, *Four Days from Fort Wingate*, p.178
[2] French, *Return to the Lost Adams Diggings*, Kindle Ed.
[3] Childress, *Lost Cities of the Southwest*, p.403.
[4] Ibid.
[5] Julyan, *Place Names of New Mexico*, p.4.

2.

GOLD BULLETS OF APACHERIA
COYOTERO APACHE GOLD

Thanks largely to the *El Paso Herald*, the Lost Adams Diggings saw a resurgence of interest in the 1920s. Old timers like William Donothan and Alvin D. Hudson added some interesting flourishes to the legend, such as that of ancient ruins carved into the canyon walls and outlaws joining with renegade Apaches to keep the diggings hidden. One of the more fantastic elements added by the *Herald* was that the Apache had slain the prospectors with golden bullets. Or, so they claimed via the headline of their February 2, 1924 issue where they proclaimed that "Indians Guard Mine With Gold Bullets; Socorro Man Has Story First Hand."

The article, in fact, was just a straight reprint of an earlier account of the diggings famously written by Socorro-area miner W.H. Byerts. And, despite what the headline claimed, no golden bullets were mentioned anywhere in the article.[1] However, tales of golden bullets had been circulating the prairies dating back to the California Gold Rush if not earlier. In retrospect, the *Arizona Republic* of April 18, 1928, remembered,

> For many years during the gold excitement in California the travelers across the open desert and through mountain passes heard the constant rumor of pioneers en route being picked off with golden bullets in the land called Arizona. They heard of the golden mystery with

doubt and feared and dreaded the uncertain journey, yet they pushed on towards the goal.

Lost Adams Diggin's

Indians Guard Mine With Gold Bullets; Socorro Man Has Story First Hand

As you can see, this article from the *El Paso Daily Herald* of February 2, 1924, made the strange claim that the Apache guarded the canyon with golden bullets.

An even earlier source, the *Pittsburgh Presbyterian Banner* of April 20, 1864, reported that,

A Navajo woman, who recently acted as guide to a party of Mexicans in a journey from the Canejo country to Santa Fe, says that in her country gold is so common that the Indians use it to make bullets. If this news is true, the whites will not be slow in exploring this Eldorado, notwithstanding the Navajo Indians and their guns loaded with golden bullets.

The main source for tales of golden bullets came from the journal of a dead man. The man was 29-year-old François Xavier Aubry, a French-Canadian merchant and early-day explorer of the Southwest. Among his best-known feats was a record-breaking horse ride from Santa Fe, New Mexico, to Independence, Missouri. (He killed several horses along the way, though.)

20

Aubry met his end in an Albuquerque bar on August 18, 1854. There, he engaged in an argument with a former politician and then-current newspaperman, Richard Hanson Weightman. When the argument escalated into a life-and-death duel, Aubry's gun misfired, and Weightman knifed him. Soon after, Aubry died, and a journal he kept of recent travels across Arizona was found.

Group of Coyotero Apache near Fort Apache, c.1873.

His journal told of how, during their travels, Aubry and his men had been besieged by the Coyotero Apache almost daily in Arizona until they finally came upon a friendly tribe willing to trade. His diary entry of the account read:

Aug. 27th. Made fifteen miles east, crossing two streams, which are branches of the Gila. We met Indians to-day, who, I think, are not Apaches Tontos as they do not speak any Spanish, and refuse to answer our questions. We obtained from them over fifteen hundred dollars' worth of gold for a few old articles of clothing. The Indians use gold bullets for their guns. They are of different sizes, and each Indian has a pouch of them. We saw an Indian load his gun with one large and three small gold bullets to shoot a rabbit. They proposed exchanging them for lead, but I preferred trading other articles. Whether the Indians made these balls themselves, or whether they were obtained by the murder of miners in California or Sonora, I am unable to say.[2]

Though many scoffed at Aubry's journal, ancillary evidence of Aubry's tales emerged in 1871, when stories began running in newspapers across the country that some prospectors had engaged in battle with a group of Apaches firing golden bullets. This occurred in a ravine north of Tucson in the summer of that year. After killing the Apache, the men found that the "pouches of the slain Indians [contained] several golden bullets, hammered out of nuggets." The blurb concluded by stating that the golden bullets confirmed the old accounts of Aubry, "whose statement with regard to the use of gold bullets was received some years ago with ridicule and doubt."[3]

THE LAND OF GOLDEN BULLETS.

A Search Going On for Mysterious Placer Mines South of San Juan.

From the Chicago Tribune.

Frederick M. Endlich of Los Angeles, Cal., is at the Grand Pacific. Mr. Endlich is erecting extensive smelting works in southern California to treat the ores of southern Nevada, southern California and Sonora, on the west coast of Mexico. He tells a romantic story of the Tonto range of mountains in the western part of Arizona, made famous about twenty years ago by the Tonto Apache Indians of that region using gold bullets in their guns. The new railroad nearly completed across these mountains from Prescott to Phœnix passes through cañons known to be rich in gold, yet no white man has ever been able to discover it.

An article published in the *Washington D.C. Evening Star* of January 27, 1893, remembered back to the days of golden bullets used by the Apache from twenty years ago, presumably referring in part to the article previously quoted from in addition to another incident. The *Evening Star* then went on to report on the capture of a solider named Surgeon Brayton, of Fort Yuma, by the Tonto Apaches.

While being held prisoner in the Tonto Mountains, he got on his captors' good side by helping to treat a malaria outbreak there. In an act of gratitude, the tribe took him to a canyon with walls that were hundreds of feet high. Through it, "a small stream of water was running" and Brayton was "allowed to work the auriferous gravel for gold." And indeed, the stream was loaded with nuggets. It stated that Brayton was familiar with tales of wounded soldiers who had bullets of gold cut from their bodies in the past, and he assumed that the canyon was the source of these golden bullets. "[Brayton] was aware that he stood upon the ground that produced these precious messengers of death."[4]

Group of Coyotero Apache and Indian Agent near Fort Apache c.1873.

Brayton did his best to ascertain the location of the canyon and managed to spy Weaver's Needle in the distance. Like Adams, Brayton escaped the Apache and endured an arduous trek through the desert until he returned to Fort Yuma with his story. Also like Adams, Brayton tried and failed in subsequent trips to find the canyon. Actually, the papers of the time thought it could have been the same bonanza found by the Adams party. The *Evening Star* stated, "It was always supposed that this gold came from the Adams region, but this was disproved during the last year."

GOLDEN BULLETS IN MEXICAN WAR

San Francisco, Calif., Oct. 4 — Bullets of solid gold were used by Yaqui Indians in fighting against Porfirio Diaz in the recent Mexican revolution, say passengers arriving here yesterday on the steamer Curacao from Mexican ports.

In Mazatlan hospitals, where many wounded underwent operations, discovery of the golden bullets, it was said, was an ordinary occurrence, although few patients received enough of them to pay the doctor bills.

This blurb, from the *Logansport Journal* of October 5, 1911, showed that the Yaqui Apache of Mexico also used golden bullets.

The paper was correct since Weaver's Needle is a good distance from the Arizona/New Mexico state line along which the diggings were said to reside. The article concluded by stating that the "country of 'golden bullets'" likely resided somewhere in the San Juan Mountain region and could potentially develop into "one of the greatest placer districts ever opened in the west."

Golden bullets would return in a haunting way in 1881 when they were used at the insistence of the notorious Coyotero Medicine man Nock-ay-det-klinne. According to an *Arizona Republic* article of April 18, 1928, Nock-ay-det-klinne was known for carrying a golden bullet on his person for good luck because it "came from the sacred space that held the spirit of his ancestors." This sacred space may have been the canyon that Brayton was allowed to see, since gold was in abundance there. However, it was also a sacred burial ground.

One day, along the flowing streams of the Cibecue, Nock-ay-det-klinne came across a lone prospector who had somehow slipped past the Apache Scouts and into their sacred lands where he was panning for gold. As Nock-ay-det-klinne watched him depart with a burro loaded with ore, he decided that he "must kill this inoffensive white man with a bullet of the metal he sought and worshipped."[5] In addition to offending the spirits of his ancestors, this prospector would possibly return with even more white men. This could not be allowed. Along the Black River at dusk, Nock-ay-det-klinne used his golden bullet to fire upon the prospector and kill him.

Nock-ay-det-klinne then took the prospector's sack of nuggets and returned them to the creek from whence they came.

According to the previously quoted *Arizona Republic* article,

Apache Medicine Man identified as "Loco".

> From time to time before the battle on the Cibicu, lone prospectors were found dead on the many trails crossing the reservation in the vicinity of Black River and in many incidents were killed with golden bullets. But little attention was paid to the circumstances due to the unsettled conditions, but it aroused a sense of wonder to many as to why such a method was necessary as the Apaches had plenty of leaden bullets, but in the turmoil and later hostile activities, isolation of the section where but few white men visited—a zone shunned by all— the unusual method of attack was forgotten...

The "turmoil and later hostile activities" the *Republic* spoke of was that of a rebellion incited by Nock-ay-det-klinne in the late summer of 1881. Nock-ay-det-klinne claimed that to help the Apache in their struggle against the White Eyes that he would raise the slain Apache chief, Diablo, from the dead.[6] Nock-ay-det-klinne also insisted that since the white man lusted after gold so much, that he should die by golden bullets.

While some of what was listed above comprised of folklore and hearsay, tensions for certain culminated in the Battle of Cibecue Creek on August 30, 1881. During the skirmish, Nock-ay-det-klinne was killed and several Apache scouts under the employ of Fort Apache mutinied to join their Coyotero brethren in battle. The historical ramifications of the fight had the White Mountain Apache leaving the reservation to join forces with Geronimo. Forgotten in the annals of history, though, was the discovery of golden bullets embedded in the bodies of the dead soldiers.

It's unknown how much truth the following paragraph contained, but the *Arizona Republic* claimed

> When the remains of the fallen soldiers were being gathered up and gently laid away in the open trench, it is reported that out of the folds of a soiled and ragged uniform of one of the victims, a golden bullet rolled to the earth. With amazement and wonder the troopers examined the crude ball, jagged and irregular in shape, but evidently serving as a yellow messenger of death.

Doctor Knew Gold Source
Knock-e-de-klinney knew the location well and its golden surroundings, for at the base of the banks of the flowing Cibicu where the remains of the departed Coyoteros rested, was the source of the golden bullets of Apacheland. He knew from tradition handed down to the doctors of mystic art, the use of the yellow metal in days gone by and its value to the whites who worshipped and fought for the golden grains.

Excerpt from the *Republic* article.

Among those who had always been fascinated by the golden bullets was Captain Sterling from Fort Apache, who prior to the rebellion had managed to befriend a Coyotero who promised to take him to the gold. The plan was for Sterling and some comrades to be guided to the spot by the friendly Coyotero, who would not proceed into the golden stream himself due to "superstitious fear."[7] The plan was to undertake the expedition in the winter of 1882. However, upon the execution of Nock-ay-det-klinne's rebellion, plans changed, and Sterling was killed in a conflict with the Apache. As the *Republic* put it, Sterling took "the secret of the location of the field of golden bullets" with him to the grave.[8]

Is it possible that the source of the golden bullets was the same hidden canyon that Surgeon Brayton of Fort Yuma saw? If you'll recall, the article that reported Brayton's story mentioned that it was once thought to be the same gold as the Adams Diggings. Many years later, in his book *Dig Here!*, Thomas Penfield resurrected the theory that the golden bullets of Cibecue were harvested from the Lost Adams, writing, "The theory has been argued that the Coyoteros' source of gold was that found by the Adams party, and then 'lost' when the prospectors were driven away by Indians."[9] Considering both Brayton's mystery canyon and that of Adams were located in Apacheria, perhaps that's where the story of the Adams Diggings being guarded by golden bullets came from?

Chapter Notes

---

[1] Tales of golden bullets circulated in the Magdelena region at one point as evidenced by a story printed in *Frontier Times* in September of 1971 entitled "Bonanza in the Mogollons" by Michael Jenkinson. The article claimed that Aubry came across the golden bullets in the Mogollon Mountains of New Mexico rather than in Arizona.

[2] Aubry, *Diary of a Journey Through Arizona*, pp.9-10.

[3] *New Bloomfield Times* (August 22, 1871).

[4] *Washington DC Evening Star* (January 27, 1893).

[5] Connell, "Golden Bullets," *Arizona Republic* (April 18, 1928).

[6] And, indeed, Ace Daklugie, son of Chief Juh, claimed that during a Ghost Dance that Nock-ay-det-klinne conjured the spirits of Mangas Coloradas, Cochise, and Victorio from the ground. Daklugie told this to Eve Ball during an interview in Ruidoso, New Mexico, in his later years.

[7] Connell, "Golden Bullets," *Arizona Republic* (April 18, 1928).

[8] Ibid.

[9] Penfield, *Dig Here!*, p.85.

THE LOST MINE.

A company of El Paso people is being organized to operate a new placer diggings in the Burro district, New Mexico.

The exact location of the grounds has not yet been announced, and the parties interested decline to give out any of the particulars for publication until all these arrangements have been perfected. It is claimed, however, that it is the old Adams diggings, which were lost many years ago.

From time to time prospecting parties from El Paso have gone out in search of the great bonanza, but the rich gold deposit was never found. It appears that in the early days a man by the name of Adams located fabulously rich placer somewhere in New Mexico north of the Texas line. Some magnificent specimens of gold were secured, including nuggets as large as beans. But the location of the deposit was lost before any great amount of gold had been taken out and the site of the mines has never been rediscovered. It is stated that while searching for the lost claims many have been killed. The Indians in that section were very unfriendly and warlike, and at least two different parties of prospectors never returned. Whether or not the old Adams diggings have been rediscovered, it is at least known that some very promising grounds have been found. A large quantity of gold dust and also a number of nuggets have been brought to El Paso and are causing great excitement. Those interesed state that they will be in a position by the latter part of this week to furnish full particulars. They now have experts on the ground.

The *Bisbee Daily Review* of August 11, 1904, made mention of the Lost Adams in relation to Gold Gulch.

3.

SKELETONS of GOLD GULCH
ANOTHER ADAMS FALSE ALARM

ocated within the confines of the Gila National Forest is a minor gold and silver placer known as Gold Gulch. The precious ores were discovered there in 1880 and small-scale mining operations began in 1883. From then until 1938 the placer was operational, though today it is only a memory. A forgotten part of Gold Gulch's legacy was that, for a time, it was a favorite "maybe" of the Lost Adams crowd.

The first tie between the Gold Gulch region and the Lost Adams came about in 1885, when members of the Sixth Cavalry came across the dead body of a prospector in the Mogollon Mountains. On his person was a letter implying that the man had been mining from the Lost Adams itself. From that point on, the soldiers asked every prospector they met along the trail if they knew the deceased miner. At the mining camp of Malone in the Burro Mountains, they found a man who said he knew this dead prospector and his partner. They had both been known to frequent Silver City and were rumored to have found a rich placer of gold. Possibly they were some of the earliest men to confuse Gold Gulch for the Lost Adams.

And why did men think Gold Gulch may have been the legendary Lost Adams? Most likely this was due to the fact that in addition to yielding gold, it also yielded the skeletons of three

GOLD STRIKE IN A CEMETERY

The Gold Gulch Excitement in Grant County Is Not Dying Out According to Reports.

AN EXPERT'S OPINION

Central People Make Important Gold Finds Near a Graveyard---Luna County Mines.

The *Santa Fe New Mexican* of October 15, 1903, reported: "The people of Central, Grant county, are excited over rich gold strikes which have been made near the cemetery of the mining camp. Wonderfully rich specimens have been found in and around the cemetery and numerous locations have been made in that vicinity. Considerable work is being done and everything points to these strikes being on a vein that is the continuation of the rich Gold Gulch vein. Several important deals have already been closed."

dead men in a cave. One of the skeletons had an old musket bearing the initials of B.F.V. Though this name doesn't appear in any Adams accounts, according to the *El Paso Herald* of May 10, 1929, B.F.V. likely stood for Benjamin F. Vorhies which the *Herald* claimed was "one of Adams' companions." The *Herald* also added, "If [the diggings were] in Gold Gulch, the story has been greatly exaggerated. For although the canyon pans out well enough under modern quantity production methods of digging, it certainly is not covered with glittering gold nuggets."[1]

A year previous to that, the *Herald* attempted some revisionist history to make Gold Gulch and the Adams Diggings one and the same. The May 7, 1928, issue of the paper, in recounting the Adams tale, specifically had Gotch Ear taking Adams and his men to a "gold gulch he knew of to the northeast." The article regurgitated the traditional Adams history before switching to the testimony of old-timer Caeser Brock, who had been living in southwestern New Mexico since 1872. It was Brock who had found the skeletons and the musket at Gold Gulch mentioned earlier.

"Around Here"

GOLD GULCH MAY BE SCENE OF LOST ADAMS DIGGIN'S

Trio Of Modern Miners Overcome ⠠⠍ Difficulties To Reach Paying Sand; Find Skeletons Of White Men In "Last Stand" Cave.

From the *El Paso Herald* of May 7, 1928.

Another source for Brock's stories about Gold Gulch and the skeletons therein was Otho Allen, who met Brock as a boy. Though Allen changed the initials etched onto the gun that Brock found, his account mostly followed Brock's reminiscences as recorded in the *El Paso Herald*. In a Federal Writer's Project interview conducted on February 25, 1938, Allen said of Brock that,

> He has a gun that is marked T. S. V. which is generally believed to belong to the Adams party. The Gold Gulch country must be where the Adams Diggings are located for Mr. Brock found the gun in a cave in the gulch. The land markings suit the Adams description.
>
> The mountain that resembles a woman's breast can be seen. I have found several 45-70 rim fire shells in the gulch, and several cradles that were made with pegs for nails. Mr. Brock used to come in with some nice nuggets and told us that he thought the gulch was where the Adams Diggings were. He later showed us the gun that he had found with the initials carved on it.
>
> There is a hole in the gulch formed by water falling from a cliff in rainy weather. In this hole one can see a heart with an arrow through it and turkey tracks in the rocks. How the Indians got in the hole to carve signs is a miracle to me. The sides of the hole are slick and curve slightly. There are many cliff dwellings around the gulch, and pit dwellings are found all along the range of mountains.

The cradle, or rocker as they were also called, that Allen spoke of was likely of Spanish origin. Evidence of Spanish mining was brought to light when cattle "pawing for water brought to light in the sandy bed of Gold Gulch an ancient 'rocker' so old that it was fastened together with pegs."[2] The fact that pegs as opposed to nails were used led to the theory it must have belonged to the Spanish. Pictured here is an example of a gold prospector pouring water through his rocker box in Pinos Altos, New Mexico, c. 1940.

Although Gold Gulch may have lived up to its name and was in the vicinity of the Adams Diggings, that certainly didn't make it so. The *El Paso Herald* of May 7, 1928, tried to explain the fact that it wasn't a perfect match for the diggings thusly,

> Although Gold Gulch as seen today bears little resemblance to the deep canyon described by Adams, there is the possible explanation that erosion has altered its sides and filled its bed.
> That erosion has filled it to a marked extent is apparent to anyone. Mr. Brock remembers when the bed was well scoured out and a stream ran along the gravel. It is so no longer. The stream bed is several feet below the surface and the water has to be brought up by a partly submerged dam as described in the foregoing.
> At the sides, the old canyon bed has been covered by erosion with slit to a varying depth, perhaps averaging

five feet. The old rocker was buried under feet of silt and sand.

Before Brock's Lost Adams theory was promoted by the *El Paso Herald* in the 1920s, in 1902 came excited claims that the Adams Diggings had been discovered near the Malone mining camp in the vicinity of Gold Gulch. *The Albuquerque Citizen* of March 19th related:

> A couple of weeks ago a party of men consisting of E.F. Heath, H. Wright, P.A. Endicott. A.D. Stout and E.L. Truitt, none of whom had ever heard of Adams and his lost diggings, started out from Lordsburg to go to Scarborough's ranch in the Burros, near which, they had heard, was some placer ground. They drove north into the Burros, lost their road, and never got to Scarborough's. Now, any one acquainted with the history of mining knows, there is no better way to find a bonanza than to get lost. They made camp, nearly froze to death that night, and the next morning found some float. They prospected up a canyon which is not far from Malone, and there found a quartz ledge, and in it free gold…

The men brought some of their samples to Lordsburg. There they told of their find in the office of the Lordsburg Liberal, and among the listeners was Don Kedzie. His Lost Adams alarm went off when he heard the men mention two red buttes near the find. Kedzie asked the men if the canyon where they discovered the gold had a little creek running through it from the buttes. When they affirmed that it did, Kedzie told them the tale of the Lost Adams, which they had never heard, and soon entered into a partnership with them. The *Arizona Republic* of March 24, 1902, also reported on the story and concluded that if "Adams was not the biggest liar on earth," perhaps the men would soon be "shipping gold out of the Burros by the carload." It noted that the find was in the vicinity of Gold Gulch and that as it had produced placer gold for years, it was a likely spot for the diggings.

> Twenty-odd years ago a man named Adams left Silver City with two friends on a prospecting trip. In the course of time he returned alone, much enfeebled in mind and body by the hardships he had encountered. He reported his two friends dead, one from an attack of Indians, the other from exposure and privation. But he brought back with him a number of fine nuggets of gold which he said he had obtained from placer ground, and which he described as situated in a gulch two days' journey from Silver City. The only landmarks he could remember were the gulch and a round-top mountain in plain sight of the same.

The above quotation, taken from the *Deming Headlight* of November 21, 1903, was referencing Adams' return expeditions to the area in the 1880s, though it conflated it with his discovery of the diggings much earlier. As you can see, the article also seemed to allude to Gold Gulch.

Unfortunately, I lost the trail of Heath, Wright, and their companions and found no further mention of them or their alleged gold. However, a slew of articles appeared in the late summer of 1903 announcing the discovery of rich veins at Gold Gulch, though none of those mentioned the Lost Adams Diggings again. How they related to the finds of the four men is unknown.

For example, the *El Paso Herald* of September 5, 1903, reported that ore found within the Gold Gulch claims would produce $440 gold to the ton and that the "new find is a short distance below the surface workings of the old Spanish mines and is believed to be another vein." The *Herald* of September 24, 1903, reported that Silver City contractor W.R. Jackson went to inspect six claims in the Gold Gulch area. The paper reported that the claims showed "wonderful production" and that when Jackson's "first car load of ore comes in he will have something to show those who have been decrying the Gold Gulch strike."

GOLD GULCH ATTRACTS
MANY MINING MEN.

Silver City, N. M., Sept. 4.—The recent big gold strike at Gold Gulch a few miles from this city has attracted quite a large number of mining men to that district. The Gold deposits continue to increase in size and from the present indications Gold Gulch will develop into one of the most promising gold camps in the southwest.

From the *Arizona Daily Star* of September 5, 1903.

Though the Lost Adams it certainly was not, Gold Gulch could have been an old Spanish mining claim as evidenced by the ancient rocker held together with pegs. Though it may have sensationalized Gold Gulch a bit, the *Border Vidette* of October 3, 1903, claimed

> Gold Gulch is the oldest gold mining camp in the United States. Long ere the advent of the Americans in New Mexico, the Spaniards mined for gold there. Numerous evidences of these old mines are conspicuous on the hillsides, tributary arroyas and gulches today. Old shafts, slopes and drifts are seen on every hand. Many of these have caved in or have been filled with debris.
>
> In many instances only the big dumps of rock, principally slate, taken from the workings, now remain to mark the site of a former Spanish gold mine. In some of these dumps are found trees which are said to be over 100 years old, denoting that operation of the mine was abandoned that long ago.

Sketch of the Burro Mountains, c. 1854.

Reports of the untold riches of Gold Gulch would be reported sporadically over the next several decades. Ultimately, Gold Gulch never produced enough gold to live up to the legend of Adams. If it played any part in the lore, perhaps it was the source of the rumors that the Spaniards had mined the Lost Adams at one time, when instead they were just mining Gold Gulch. Furthermore, it would seem that the *El Paso Herald*, looking for a new angle on the Lost Adams, simply decided to resurrect the claims of Caeser Brock for the sake of a new story on the diggings, which were always good to sell papers.

Chapter Notes

---

[1] *El Paso Herald* May 10, 1929.
[2] *El Paso Herald*, May 7, 1928.

4.

FORT WINGATE GOLD
SAN RAFAEL TREASURE

As alluded to in the previous chapter, the Lost Adams Diggings were occasionally linked to the Spanish conquistadors, the thought being that perhaps they, too, mined Sno-Ta-Hay Canyon in the past. Somewhere near the lava-scarred malpais in northwestern New Mexico lies a Spanish treasure trove, the story of which occasionally bled into the Adams Diggings. How exactly the two tales became intertwined is simple. When Adams was found half-dead wandering through the desert, in most iterations of his story, he was taken to Fort Wingate to recover. And, since Fort Wingate also played into the story of the Spanish gold, the two tales naturally conjoined over time.

However, before recounting the legend, it's important to differentiate the current placement of Fort Wingate from its original location. In 1862, what was called Fort Wingate—in reality just an encampment and not a permanent structure—was located at a locale known as Ojo del Gallo. The presence of the soldiers and the safety they fostered encouraged settlers to move to the area. When the soldiers left for a permanent location forty miles to the northwest, the Hispanic settlement became known as San Rafael.

Survey camp near Fort Wingate, probably not dissimilar to the Fort Wingate encampment of 1862 at San Rafael. (T.H. O'Sullivan, c.1873)

In the vicinity of San Rafael was a mesa, on top of which supposedly was buried a Spanish gold horde. The gold dated back to the Pueblo Revolt of 1680, when the Puebloans overthrew their Spanish overlords and drove them out of the Kingdom of New Spain. During the Spaniards' mass exodus of what is now New Mexico, a large mining operation had to be abandoned in the San Mateo Mountains (located in current-day Socorro County). Not coincidentally, the mountains formed the eastern border of the Plains of San Agustin, often considered as a possible location for the Lost Adams.

A Franciscan friar was put in charge of seven soldiers to sneak back into the old mine and pack up as much of the gold as possible, which they did on eighteen pack mules. During their travels, they found themselves accosted by Indians, the tribe of which has never been specified. The group sought the high ground of the mesa above current-day San Rafael. There they buried their gold, then, free of their burdensome cargo, fought off their attackers and made an escape. Eventually, the tribe caught up to the party, killing all but one or two who managed to escape to El Paso, where they told their tale.

Apacheria Gold

Contrary to many fantastical treasure tales, this one had some evidence to back it up. In a 1935 deathbed confession, an old sheepherder told of finding gold atop the mesa and produced one ingot as proof. When this encouraged the other villagers of San Rafael to go looking for the gold, they found the grave of a Spanish soldier on the mesa, who they disinterred and reburied in the San Rafael cemetery.

Indian reservation near McCartys, New Mexico, which is situated not too far from San Rafael, c. March, 1943. (Jack Delano, Library of Congress)

Considering San Rafael was the original location of Fort Wingate, where Adams once stayed, it should come as no surprise that the Adams Diggings sometimes bled into the San Rafael gold legend.[1] A good example of this is "SOME LOST FORTUNES" published in the *Phoenix Arizona Republican* on January 2, 1900. In the article, Elfreth Watkins Jr. told of a lost treasure tale taking place between Grants and McCartys, which would fit San Rafael perfectly. The tale peppered in a few elements of the Lost Adams, notably a lone survivor of the ordeal.[2] For some reason, Watkins moved the time period from the 1680s to the 1850s, long after the conquistadors had left New Mexico. Lastly, it also specified that the attacking tribe was the Navajo, noteworthy because many Lost Adams renditions told in the early 1900s had replaced the Apache with the Navajo. With those details in mind, the relevant portions of the account were as follows:

When the California gold rush was at its height, many Mexicans were tempted to try their luck in the new El Dorado. One of their expeditions, which had met with tremendous success was returning home with a large burro train weighed down with gold, and was following a trail leading past the spot mentioned, when they heard that a great band of Navajos were about to raid them.

The burros were immediately stripped of their costly burden and all hands set to work to hide it in the earth, hoping for sufficient time to escape before the Indians might arrive.

Not until after the last nugget had been securely covered, certain markers had been planted, and preparations had been made for rapid flight, did the poor Mexicans realize that their time had been ill reckoned.

The Navajos, who greatly outnumbered their victims, swept in upon their band and slaughtered all but one, who fled in terror to a settlement beyond, where, in great excitement, he told his tale and left a meager description of the hiding place. Hurrying in search of others to help him recover the gold, this man evidently met with some mishap on the way.

At any rate, he never returned, but certain Mexicans, to whom the story was confided, hurried to find the place designated. After excavating many feet, one of these men hit with his shovel a stone with peculiar markings, which resounded with such a weirdly hollow tap as to lend him to believe that something uncanny resided beneath. He fled from the spot, alarming his companions, who, being a superstitious people, imagined that in a cavern beneath the soil ghosts of the massacred miners were watching as sentries over their lost treasure.

After this incident the spot became forgotten, as none of the superstitious diggers could be induced to return. But the story still lived. The source of my information is such as to lead me to suspect the truth.

Fort Wingate from a distance.

William Donothan, who was a sergeant in the Seventh Cavalry, claimed to have heard tales of Spaniards mining the Lost Adams before Adams. Specifically, he said that the Apache claimed that the Spaniards would venture into the malpais and return with wagonloads of gold. On one such excursion, the Apache massacred a Spanish wagon train of gold and burned the wagons. Donothan claimed to have found remnants of the massacre in the malpais in the form of old charred wagons, and embedded in the burned wood were arrowheads.

The San Rafael gold story could possibly be related to Donothan's account of Spaniards in the malpais with gold. In

More Mysteries & Miracles of New Mexico, author Jack Kutz provided a variation of the San Rafael tale that matched Donothan's findings. Rather than burying the cache atop the mesa, some of the gold-carrying burros ran off into the malpais during the attack. Yet another version had the Spanish gold train attacked and killed in the malpais.

Likewise, a 1927 excursion to find the Adams Diggings turned up a few anecdotes relating to San Rafael. The participants asked an old-time prospector from Grants about gold stories, though they didn't mention the Lost Adams specifically as they were trying to keep their expedition a secret. The old prospector responded that just a few weeks ago, a Zuni man had come out of the hills just below San Raphael and came into town where he purchased items from the local store using "a gold nugget as big as a Hen's egg." When they asked him where he got the gold, he would only point towards the malpais and say, "Far in hills, much danger for white men."[3] Though the presumption among the Adams hunters of 1927 was that the gold came from Sno-Ta-Hay Canyon, perhaps it really came from the mesa above San Rafael.

Although the Lost Adams Diggings and the Spanish gold allegedly buried atop San Rafael Mesa certainly comprise different treasures, due to their close proximity, it's likely both legends have influenced one another over the years and thus also confused both accounts.

Chapter Notes

[1] Of course, in the pre-internet age, most everything was hearsay, so it's only natural that storytellers mistakenly fused together unrelated stories every so often.

[2] In the traditional San Rafael account more than one man survived.

[3] Phillips, "A Pilot's Opinion of the Lost Adams," *Gold!* (Fall 1975), p.36.

5.

AZTEC GOLD OF ADAMS CAVE
THE SAGA OF ADAMS, THE SECOND

Throughout the mid-1870s and into the end of the 1880s, it wasn't uncommon for a disheveled man known as Adams to wander into Fort Defiance. As usual, he was returning more dead than alive from another failed venture to find a lost canyon leading to a bonanza of gold. The only problem was the canyon was always guarded by Indians.

I speak not of the Adams who lacked a first name, but a lesser-known successor named Henry Adams. Though they shared the same last name and a similar story, they presented separate, though possibly related incidents. While the more famous Adams found Apache gold not far from Fort Wingate, this Adams was shown Navajo gold within the Navajo reservation nearest Fort Defiance in Arizona. Though exact dates are never given in the case of Henry Adams, it would seem his first encounter with the gold occurred in the 1870s, though tales of what was later deemed "Adams Cave" didn't become widely circulated until the turn of the century.

I was first alerted to this story via an article published in the *Boston Daily Globe* on October 23, 1900. Initially fearing it was a one-off invented by the *Globe* to entertain eastern readers, I luckily found about half a dozen other articles on the subject. Like the Lost Adams, each told the tale from a different perspective and, to a lesser degree, included conflicting details. What follows is not a pastiche but a conglomeration of the articles. Unfortunately, none of them included precise dates for when Henry Adams first found Adams Cave, which the papers acted as though was just as famous as the Lost Adams Diggings. Actually, many accounts seemed to think that Adams Cave was synonymous with the diggings.

"Aboriginal life among the Navajoe Indians. Near old Fort Defiance, N.M.," c.1873 by T.H. O'Sullivan.

------◇------

SEARCH FOR ADAMS' CAVE

Tragedy of One of Arizona's Lost Mines.

Every district of the mining country of the west has it own story of a lost mine, says the New York Sun. Lonely prospectors have wandered away into the mountains and the deserts of the southwest and have returned after days of absence to cautiously display samples of fabulously rich ore, discovered somewhere in their wanderings. From one cause and another they have disappeared later and with them has vanished every trace of the rich deposits of the precious metal that they have discovered. Others have taken the fever from the glimpse they had of the shining specimens and have gone in quest of the shining treasure. They were powerless in the grasp of the prospector's eternal hope. They followed to the hills or the deserts and died on the sands of the alkiline waste or in giant crevices or in deep canyons of the mountains. Not until these give up their dead will it be known how many have perished in the search for the lost mines of the west.

Another article on "Adams Cave," printed in the *Phoenix Arizona Republican* of August 11, 1900.

45

The *Mitchell Daily Republican* of April 24, 1902, called Adams Cave "the most famous of all the lost treasures of the west." It continued that "For more than twenty years [Henry] Adams has searched for the cave, and the story of his adventures would fill a volume." It also stated, "For nearly a century Arizona and New Mexico miners have told the story of the great treasure hidden away in the hills of the Navajo reservation."

The Navajo at Fort Defiance.

The best place to start the tale is probably with the *Phoenix Arizona Republican* of August 11, 1900, which explained, "Shortly after the Indians had been crowded back into the district they now occupy [in the 1880s], and the government had sent out its soldiers to keep them there, a man named Henry Adams came out from the east and established a little trading store at Ft. Defiance." Interestingly, it also noted that Adams "cared little or nothing for the trade of the white men, and few, if any, outside of the soldiers ever came to his store."

According to the *Boston Daily Globe* piece, Adams was alerted to the gold's existence when three Navajo braves came in "with a bag of golden nuggets to purchase extensive outfits for the tribe" from his trading post.[1] Within a week they returned, this time with gold dust to serve as their currency. Odder yet, the next specimen the Navajo brought in was described as "a small ingot of pure gold, marked with strange characters."

Knowing the Navajo couldn't leave the reservation, Adams surmised that the gold had to have come from somewhere on the reservation. As Adams became better acquainted with the three Navajo braves, he finally asked them the source of their gold, which they initially would not divulge. However, eventually, they consented. According to the *Republican* version of the tale, at twilight the three men rode out of Fort Defiance with

FAMOUS LOST MINE HAS BEEN FOUND

Harry C. Adams' Long Search for Cavern Treasures Has Been Rewarded.

COST UNCLE HIS LIFE

Sent His Brother Directions for Finding Location of Place of Wealth— An Adventurous Nephew Continued Search.

Houck's Tank, Ariz., April 24.—Harry C. Adams, formerly of Pittsburg, Pa., and T. D. Hardson of Salem, O., with a party of Navajo guides, reached here a few days ago with a remarkable story of the discovery of Adams cave, the most famous of all the lost treasures of the west.

The *Mitchell Daily Republican* of April 24, 1902.

Adams. Their journey lasted all night until they arrived at the mouth of a canyon at dawn. Before going any further, the Navajo insisted that Adams be blindfolded for the rest of the trip. The distance from the entrance to the canyon and the mouth of the cave differed between the two articles slightly, with the *Republican* noting it as one or two miles and the *Globe* describing it as one or two hours. In any case, at the mouth of the cave, per the *Republican*,

> The horses were tied and Adams was led up the side of a steep hill, still blindfolded, and into a cave. The air was damp and cool, as though the cavern extended far back into the mountain. The Indians removed the bandage and invited Adams to look about him. The floor of the cave was littered with gold—nuggets and ingots; it seemed to be the hiding place for the old races of Mexico, who, it was said, had come this far north in their effort to secrete their treasures from the Spaniards.

The *Globe's* version of the cave was basically the same, but will be reprinted here for enthusiasts that would like to note the differences:

> They rode an hour or two longer, and then [Adams] felt that they had entered a cave, for the air was cool and damp. They stopped, dismounted, walked a short distance and removed the blind.
>
> Henry Adams never forgot the sight he then beheld. He was, he declared afterward, in a great rocky cavern or vault, half a hundred feet in height, twice as many wide and almost circular. It was lighted by torches carried by his guides. These showed under his feet and all over the floor gold dust and gold nuggets strewn in profusion. Piled against the walls were broken, rotted wooden chests, through holes in which showed dull yellow ingots of gold.
>
> Adams looked in amazement and awe. He realized that he had found the great treasure of the Aztecs, brought north and hidden to escape the Spanish rapine. He begged to be allowed to take some of the ingots away, but the Indians refused, and turned to blindfold him again.
>
> As they did so he caught a glimpse of daylight through the entrance, and far away of three peaks, exactly alike, and standing side by side.

Upon his return to Fort Defiance, Adams had the "phantom gold fever"[2] and became obsessed with finding the treasure horde. Luckily, he also found a keen disciple in the form of a man named Judge Griscom, "who shared his enthusiasm and financed further expeditions."[3]

The *Republican* related the ensuing years:

> The search was continued for three years. Nearly every portion of the reservation was gone over by the prospector. At the end of that time, although the judge had become discouraged and had ceased to help Adams, and the others of whom he secured aid had followed

suit, the man who had seen the treasure was as confident and enthusiastic as ever. He fitted out several expeditions himself; was wounded again and at last returned helplessly bankrupt and ruined in health to Tucson, to again enlist the aid of Judge Griscom. The judge listened patiently to all Adams had to say, but in the end he replied that he could no longer furnish funds for the search. Adams begged and pleaded with him. "There is only a small portion of the whole reservation left unexplored," he insisted. "The treasure is no where else; it must be there."

But the judge was obdurate; he would not yield. Adams determined to make his way to Phoenix and there attempt to persuade his old friend, a man named Spangler, to fit out a final expedition. He mounted the stage bound for Phoenix, but before he left the town he heard of Spangler's death. Adams remained in the vehicle; as it turned the corner of the long white road that leads away to Phoenix, darkness came down suddenly, as it does on the western plains. The driver heard the door open, turned in time to see a man spring from the slowly moving coach, saw a flash of steel and heard the report that followed. Grown weary with the long search, at last discouraged and disheartened, Adams had placed the muzzle of the gun to his forehead and fired the shot that killed him.

Just outside of Tucson a little rude monument, with the name of Adams scrawled with uncertain characters over its surface, stands half buried in the drifting sands. Beneath it lies the first man who perished in search for "Adams Cave;" the resting places of the scores of others who have given up their lives in the search for the lost treasure will never be known until the seas of salty sand give up their secrets and their dead.

However, this is by far the end of the story. The article failed to mention that before his death in 1898, Adams had written to his brother in Pennsylvania, giving a detailed account of the treasure cave. Adams requested that if he should die, then his brother (name not given) should continue the search.[4] To that end, he sent along maps of the country with directions for finding the cave. "The brother preferred to remain on the farm, but his more adventurous son started out to follow up the wealth of his uncle," one article explained. Though many articles were written on the ensuing treasure hunt, the *Mitchell Daily Republican* of April 24, 1902, best explained the efforts of Henry Adam's nephew to find the gold. His name was Harry Adams, of Pittsburgh, Pennsylvania, and along with him came his friend, T. D. Hardson, of Salem, Ohio.

With young Hardson, [Adams] fitted out an expedition at Albuquerque and went into the Navajo country. Scores of times they met hostile Indians, and after searching for several years were forced to leave the country, the Navajos following them nearly to Fort Defiance.

They spent a number of years in various struggles again to get back into the reservation. But each time they were driven out until about two years ago. A government order [two years ago] was then issued opening the reservation to prospectors providing the Indians were given a certain percentage of any valuable ore that might be found.

Adams and Hardson at once returned to their search and with a party of Indian guides scoured the country. Three weeks ago in following up a deep wash in the Tunicha mountains they came upon a cave in a canyon's side. From the mouth of the cave the three peaks mentioned in the old papers left by Adams could plainly be seen. In half an hour they had penetrated to the end of the cavern. On the floor of the cave they failed to find the gold nuggets and ingots, as described by the original finder of the cave, the Indians probably having carried most of them away. But far back in the hole they discovered another crevice, and crawling up through that they came upon a shaft of what was apparently an abandoned mine.

Strewn about the surface were stone hammers and mauls and chunks of ore glittering with gold. Hardson, at a rope's end, clambered down the shaft to find an immense ledge of gold ore penetrated by tunnels and shafts.

Gathering some of the best specimens of gold the party hurried away, leaving guards at the cave.

An expedition is now being fitted out at Holbrook and men are being engaged for heavy operations at the mine. The old gold mine will soon be equipped with modern machinery.

FOUND THE AZTEC TREASURE.

Isaac Thurlow Claims He Knows Where Millions Are Hidden.

A gray-haired, weather-beaten old man named Isaac Thurlow has recently arrived in Chicago from Arizona. He makes the extraordinary claim that he has located the lost mine of the Aztecs.

He admits that he is not the pioneer in this search for the Aztecs' wealth. A man named Henry Adams of Fort Defiance, Ari, had his cupidity aroused through some reservation Indians coming to his store with a bag of golden nuggets to purchase extensive outfits for the tribe; and he, years ago, determined to find it.

Boston Daily Globe of October 23, 1900.

If Adams Cave was thoroughly mined thereafter, I can find no record of it, and its final fate is unknown. So far, all Adams Cave has left in its wake are dangling threads, among them Henry Adams' speculation that the source of the treasure was Aztec gold taken north to evade the Spaniards. This wasn't an idea completely out of left field. For years, stories circulated about a procession of Aztecs who escaped the Spanish invasion and returned to their homeland in the north. And there they stored their gold to prevent it from falling into the hands of their enemies. However, the final destination of this Aztec treasure caravan has spanned the entirety of the Southwest from Utah to Texas. Adams Cave is, therefore, only one of many possibilities for the Aztec gold repository.

Another dangling thread of Adams Cave is its nebulous connection to the Lost Adams Diggings. As it was, towards the end of the 19th century, many Adams hunters thought Sno-Ta-Hay Canyon resided on Navajo land instead of within Apacheria. Adams Cave fit the bill as it resided on Navajo land and had to be accessed through a small canyon, just like the diggings. Henry Adams' sighting of three peaks coincided somewhat with the two peaks that the other Adams often spoke of as well. However, all that said, Adams Cave was most likely a different treasure cache despite the similarities.

In the end, only one thing is certain, while Adams Cave is now largely forgotten, the legend of the Lost Adams lives on.

Chapter Notes

[1] Interestingly, a few of the members of a treasure forum had noted the difficulty in finding an Adams Trading Post at Fort Defiance. One of them speculated that perhaps Adams had a small operation, and the article in the *Phoenix Arizona Republican* of August 11, 1900, would seem to allude to this when it described Adams "sitting in the shade of his rude 'shack'" when three Navajo braves came in to purchase items using gold nuggets. I did at least find mention of Henry Adams in an academic paper unrelated to lost treasure, though, so he did exist. In "Blood and Ice: Intimacy and Factionalism at Fort Defiance Indian Agency, 1887–1888" by David Wallace Adams (*Western Historical Quarterly*, Volume 50, Issue 3, Autumn 2019), Henry Adams was mentioned as the acting Indian agent in 1887 in the absence of another officer. *The Miner* of October 11, 1878, also mentioned a Henry Adams and a posse of men pursuing the perpetrators of a stagecoach robbery near Date Creek, Arizona. However, Date Creek is a long way from Fort Defiance, though Adams could have been in the Date Creek area for a time and moved to Fort Defiance later.

[2] *Boston Daily Globe* (October 23, 1900).

[3] Ibid.

[4] However, one has to ask, if Adams felt his brother might help, then why did he kill himself?

RED HILL TREASURE

ANOTHER ADAMS AT PINOS ALTOS

There are several towns along the border of western New Mexico with strong ties to the Adams Diggings. Many prospectors, for instance, used either Grants, Magdalena, or Silver City as starting points on their searches. A few miles north of Silver City, though, is one village in particular with strong ties to the diggings, that being Pinos Altos. This is because one of the settlement's founders was Colonel Jacob Snively, likely the real persona behind the mysterious Dutchman in the Adams party.

Like Adams and his varying first names, many different men were speculated to be "the Dutchman," but Snively lined up the best for most researchers. He certainly fit the bill of "old Indian fighter" as he was described in some iterations of the Adams saga. In 1837, Snively served as an ambassador to the Shawnee Indians on behalf of what was then the Republic of Texas and eventually retired from the army as a Colonel. In 1849, he became one of the California Gold Rush 49ers and in the next decade he was in New Mexico finding gold. Actually, Snively seemed to have a knack for discovering gold all across the Southwest, and his exploits could fill a book all their own.

Snively arrived at what would be Pinos Altos in 1860 with a few other prospectors. A companion of his by the name of Birch discovered gold in a stream. As such, for a time the place was called Birchville before becoming Pinos Altos, or *tall pines*, in 1866. It was at Pinos Altos in 1865 that Snively arrived with a mule loaded with $10,000 worth of gold, which many suspect came from the Lost Adams. Perhaps to protect himself and the location of the gold, Snively never told a story similar to that of the Adams Diggings of a party of white prospectors massacred by the Apache. As such, his gold was often called the Snively Diggings, though many Adams hunters, like Jason Baxter and Jack Purcell, suspected they were one and the same.

A narrow-gauge railroad to the mines at Pinos Altos. (Forest Service)

In addition to being founded by a suspected member of the Adams party, Pinos Altos also hosted a lost treasure tale involving a man known only as Adams. He was not, however, the same Adams and nor was the treasure that of the diggings. Called the "Red Hill Treasure," as is common with such stories, the dates given to this tale often conflicted. Historian Marc Simmons listed it as being found towards the end of the 19th century and said that the prospector named Adams was hunting Snively's lost gold. However, more numerous sources placed it in the late 1830s, which was somewhat odd considering New Mexico was under Mexican rule at that time.[1]

Pinos Altos c.1900, many years after the story in this chapter occurred. (Taken from *The Pinos Altos Story* by Dorothy Watson)

In any case, the story went that an old prospector known only as Adams came staggering into a mining camp in the vicinity of what would later be Pinos Altos. The man was riddled with arrow wounds and bullet holes alike from an Indian attack and looked to be on his last leg. On his deathbed, he told of discovering placer gold in a stream within sight of a distinctive red hill. Further upstream, he found gold nuggets, which he began stuffing in his saddlebag. About then the Apache came calling and attacked him, and the man had barely made it out of the wilderness alive. With his dying breath, the old prospector pointed to the north, saying the red hill was about two or three days in that direction. After that, Adams died, and the prospectors pondered if his tale was one of many that would go unsubstantiated. To their shock, when they found the old man's horse, it was carrying a saddlebag with about 25 pounds of gold that later totaled $7,000. Some said that Pinos Altos sprang from this event, though that is not the case. However, the tale of the "Red Hill Treasure" did entice fortune hunters to look for the distinctive landmark, which Marc Simmons said had a "reddish glow" due to the carmine soil on its slopes.[2]

Sometime between 1920 and 1930, a settlement popped up between Springerville and Quemado called Red Hill. Naturally, the name was chosen because of a red hill that could be seen north of town. Once, while digging out some rain reservoirs, gold was found in the earth. However, no gold was apparently ever found on the red hill north of the town itself, so it's unknown if it was the same landmark related to the lost gold of Adams.

Chapter Notes

[1] There are records of a mining settlement there under Mexican rule, by the way, and Anglo prospectors roamed the region from time to time.

[2] Simmons, *Treasure Trails of the Southwest*, p.120.

7.

JUH'S GOLD

LOST "SQUAW MINE" OF SANTA RITA

Ask anyone about Geronimo and most will respond that he was an Apache chief. And while Geronimo was a fierce Apache warrior and medicine man, he was actually never a chief. Instead, Geronimo often served under his close friend, Chief Juh, a brilliant military strategist.

Juh was a large man, standing over six feet tall and was thought to weigh over 220 pounds. Like his confidant Geronimo, Juh possessed a supernatural ability that the Apaches quantified as "Power." The "Power" was acquired after a four-day fast in the wilderness, seeking communion with the one god of the Apache, Ussen. Many Apache, especially the warrior woman Lozen and also Geronimo, had the Power of foresight. Juh had this as well, and even his name meant *He sees ahead.* Juh's son, Ace Daklugie, explained his power to Eve Ball, stating,

> Juh, my father, had great Powers—several of them. Like Geronimo, he could foretell the future. That is what his name means: he sees ahead. But the greatest of all his Power was to handle men. No Apache had to perform compulsory military service. No warrior got pay for fighting. My father told his men that he could offer them nothing but death.[1]

Son of Juh, Ace Daklugie.

And indeed, Juh did have Power over men, as he successfully negotiated a peace treaty between his tribe and President Díaz himself in Mexico. He also executed some of the most successful military attacks in Apacheria against the U.S. cavalry. Nor did Juh surrender or die at the cavalry's hands. Juh died September 21, 1883, in Chihuahua, Mexico, when he suffered a heart attack and fell off his horse.

Dan Thrapp, the respected Apache historian, wrote *Juh: An Incredible Indian* and said this of the chief:

> During his mature life, Juh, a redoubtable Apache and a man with a talent for war, was closely associated with and overshadowed by Geronimo. But Juh was a chief and Geronimo only a war leader; Juh took precedence over his warrior comrade and Geronimo deferred to Juh. That is how history should rank these two redoubtable Apache leaders, but until recently the record has been reversed.[2]

Ace Daklugie, right, acting as translator for Geronimo, center.

As all treasure enthusiasts know, Nana had the Lost Adams, Geronimo had his hidden gold cache, and Victorio had the gold-laden peak bearing his name within White Sands Missile Range. Just as Juh was a lesser-known chief, he also had a lesser-known treasure trove to his name located somewhere in the Santa Rita Mountains outside of Silver City. However, it was likely fool's gold. The *Las Cruces Rio Grande Republican* of April 29, 1910, ran the story "The Original Tale of Treasure Trove in Grant County."

The story began excitingly, with Juh holding up "an ore train in northern Mexico, bound from one of the rich mines of the Yaqui district to Chihuahua..." Juh and his braves secured about $40,000 worth of ore from the train. After giving a share to his men, Juh set off alone with five squaws, forbidding any of the men to follow him. They rode north towards New Mexico Territory and after crossing the Gila River, Juh and the women entered Greenwood Canyon, about thirty miles northwest of Silver City. The paper noted that at the time, the unnamed canyon was a "favorite rendezvous of Mangas Coloradas and other chiefs…"

The story took an ominous turn when the paper quoted from a man who claimed to know the lone survivor of the group of women who accompanied Juh to the canyon:

Here the squaw says he deposited the bullion beneath one of the overhanging cliffs with which the canyon is bordered and then he sealed the cliff. This done, he took his war club and beat the five squaws in the head. The old woman was left for dead among her four companions but after laying unconscious for several hours, she came to and found aid among the friendly Apaches that infested the section at that time. After Geronimo's capture, she settled in Santa Rita and from there drifted to the Mesilla valley where the descendants of some of her tribe lived. The old woman could never be induced to go back to the scene of the hidden treasure for fear she would be captured by the enraged Jhu (Hoo) or some of his descendants for revealing the tale and she continues to believe this section of the country is the home of the Apache braves of yore, despite the most urgent representation of her friends that the Indians have been driven from the country arid that she would be perfectly safe in making the trip.

It's likely that Juh did no such thing, and the old woman was telling a tall tale for reasons unknown. For that matter, this went beyond being a secondhand story. It was brought to the *Silver City Enterprise* by a local man, M.F. Fleming, who had heard it from a "Col. Van Potten," who was by then deceased. The paper said that Van Potten was a former employee of the Las Cruces Land Office and one "of the pioneers of this section" who was "very influential among the Indian and Mexican residents on the Mesilla valley." It was Van Potten who heard of the "aged Indian woman living in the valley who was telling a strange tale of a treasure trove hidden in the mountains near Santa Rita." Van Potten went to verify the woman's story, and according to Fleming, that was what she told Van Potten.

The story of Juh's gold is an obscure one. If it was better known, I have a feeling Eve Ball would have asked Juh's son, Ace Daklugie, about it. Had she done so, Daklugie would probably have confirmed that Juh's killing of the four women was a lie.

Chapter Notes

---

1 Ball, *Indeh*, p.61.
2 Thrap, *Juh*, back matter.

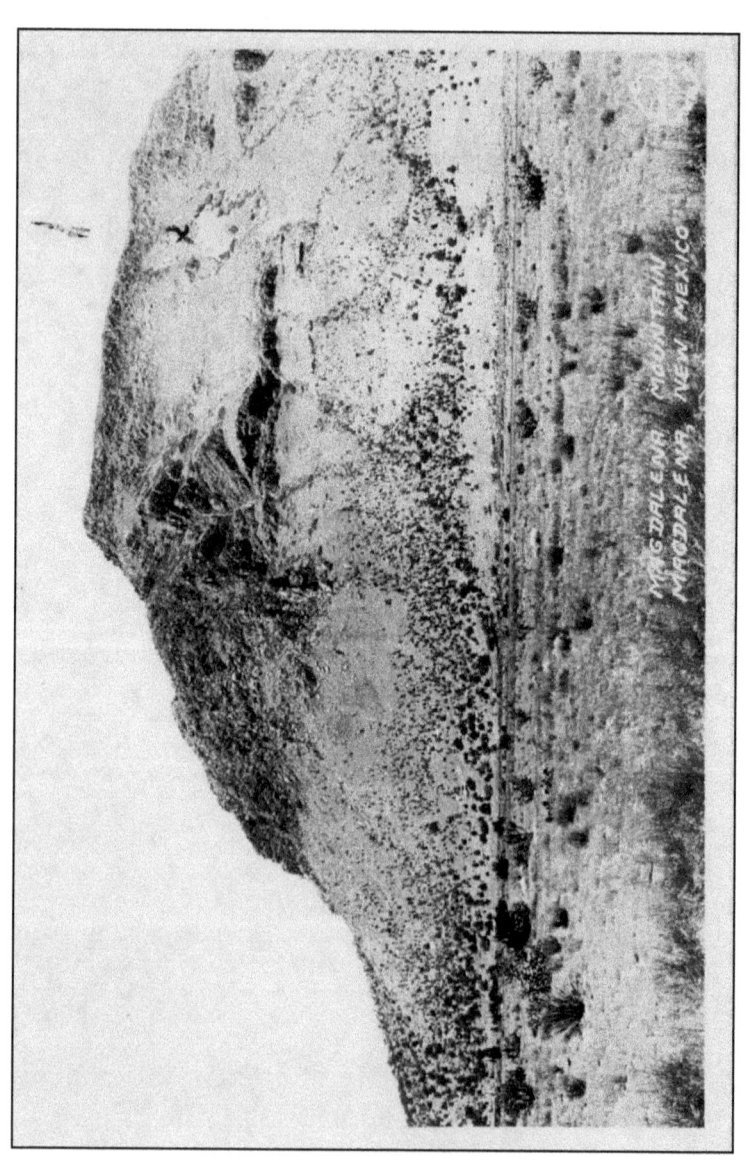

MAGDALENA MOUNTAIN
MAGDALENA NM, NEW MEXICO

8.

LADY of MAGDALENA

LEGENDS OF A NOTABLE LANDMARK

Among the landmarks pointing the way to the Lost Adams, the most important was undoubtedly a pair of twin peaks within sight of the diggings. The most romantic, however, was easily the Lady of Magdalena. This mountain, for which the town of Magdalena was named, bears on its face the profile of a woman. Actually, whether or not this was the mountain that Adams searchers saw on their desert treks is debatable, but many accounts spoke of a mountain resembling a woman in some way.

It was Adams hunter Jason Baxter who made the strongest claims linking the Lady of Magdalena to the Lost Adams. Baxter was relating the story of a German cook who had stumbled across the diggings to James McKenna. In Mckenna's book, *Black Range Tales*, Baxter was quoted as saying that the man located the diggings in the vicinity of "a mountain with a woman's picture painted on it in bright colors, but where it was he could not tell."[1] Baxter felt certain that it was in the vicinity of Magdalena since there was a mountain there featuring what looked like the profile of a woman on its side:

> On the east slope of the mountain the head of a woman can be made out without any trouble. The shrubs on the mountainside have grown around a rocky outcroppin' and it sure does look like woman's face. This mound of many colors and it's lonesome settin' stirred up good

feelin' in the Spaniards, and they called it our Lady of Magdalena. The mountain is located near the north end of the Black Range, close to the edge of the San Augustine Plains.[2]

Baxter also claimed that the Lady of Magdalena was a sacred spot for the Apache. According to Baxter, there had never been a murder committed in close proximity to the mountain. "Even an Apache will not kill an enemy if he can get within the shadow of the woman's face," Baxter claimed.[3]

Lady Magdalena, Near Magdalena, N. M.
Copyright by W. M. Borrowdale.

Baxter was referring to a popular area legend that concerned a small band of conquistadors that had branched off from the main group to go their own way up the Rio Grande valley.[4] Eventually, they found themselves on the run from Apache. Exhausted and out of provisions, they took it as a good sign when they came upon a mountain with the face of a woman in its side. Not only that, it seemed that their Apache pursuers would not harm them under the face of the mountain. A more fanciful version of the legend also existed, which stated that the face on the mountain brightened and appeared at the very moment the Apache began to attack. Seeing the divine form, the Apache fled.

An alternative to the "mountain with the face of a woman" could've been the Kneeling Nun located in the Santa Rita Mountains near Silver City. Baxter claimed that a "Mexican half-breed" (not implied to be Gotch Ear, by the way) told him the Kneeling Nun formed shortly after the Spaniards set up a monastery in the area. When one of the nuns broke her vows, she was turned to stone as punishment, or so the legend went.

After the encounter, the men recalled a legend from Spain relating to Mary Magdalene, who, it was said, spent her last days in penance and prayer atop a mountain. After her death, it was said that the face of a beautiful woman appeared on the mountain. Henceforth, in Spain, it was known as La Sierra de Maria Magdalene. And so it was in the Kingdom of New Spain as well, as many think that's how the peak got its name.

From that point forward, the spot became a place of refuge from Indian attacks for settlers, Anglo and Spanish alike. F.A. Jones wrote in *New Mexico Mines and Minerals*:

> This spot became a place of refuge and the savage Indian would forego his bloody deeds under the shadow of the holy mount. Those in danger would flee to this enchanted spot and thus become invulnerable from the onslaught of their pursuers.[5]

During Geronimo's raids on the area in the mid-1880s, a Magdalena old-timer, Vivian V. Clark, claimed that hundreds of area residents took refuge under the face of the mountain due to the belief that the Indians revered it. Whether that was the case or not, Geronimo and his band never came calling at the foot of the mountain.

Geronimo at Socorro.

One could argue that the mountain became the guardian angel of the village of Kelly, located nearest the mountain. The old frontier writer—but not the frontier fighter himself—Kit Carson said in *Frontier Times* that "by strange reasons" Kelly was "never attacked during its many years as a mining town."[6] Carson went on to state that the Apache "feared the mountain and the symbols formed on its sides" and that they "believed that should they ever cause blood-spill within the shadows of the mountain, the wrath of their God would bring destruction upon the entire tribe."[7]

Carson noted that

> Any enemy of the Apache, whether miner, rancher, or trader, when suffering from the ravages of their attacks, always considered himself safe—and was—when he reached Kelly. Many a frontiersman and his family escaped death at the hands of the Indians by making a mad dash for the mining town.

At a certain point, the marauders always halted their ferocious onslaught and retreated. The miners knew it and always raced to that zone for safety.[8]

Carson claimed that the Lady of Magdalena "allowed millions of dollars' worth of ore to be dug from the hills unmolested"[9] due to the Apache superstition about the mountain—whatever it was. Sadly, we still don't know just why the Apache held the mountain sacred, unless, of course, it was simply for the same reason that the Spanish did.

Chapter Notes

[1] McKenna, *Black Range Tales*, p.36.
[2] Ibid, p.37.
[3] Ibid, p.61.
[4] Danita Ross covered the Lady of Magdalena in *The Santa Fe New Mexican* of June 24, 1983. In her article she related, "Legend claims that Spaniards following Coronado's quest for the Seven Cities walled in gold, named the image, seeing it as a holy sign of good fortune soon to come to them." If that is indeed the case, then there is another gold-linked legend for the Lady of Magdalena to claim.
[5] Jones, *New Mexico Mines and Minerals*, p.119.
[6] Carson, "The Shadow of Magdalena," *Frontier Times* (Aug/Sep 1963), p.26.
[7] Ibid.
[8] Ibid.
[9] Ibid, p.27.

A SINGULAR STORY.

THE APACHE CHIEF, COCHISE, AND HIS
FATHER—THE GOLDEN MOUNTAIN AND
THE SACRED LEGEND—MASONRY AMONG
THE APACHES.

In the Fall of 1870, writes a correspondent, while sitting on the porch of
the hotel in Santa Fe, New Mexico, a
party of twelve horsemen approached.
Their horses were jaded and gaunt as
from a long and difficult journey. The
riders were dressed in buckskin overshirts, cavalry pants, heavy boots and
large Mexican spurs. Dismounting at
the hotel, the horses and men were
cared for. A tall, slim, hickory-iron
sort of a man, who seemed to be leader,
made arrangements aside with the landlord. After supper, falling into conversation with the leader of the party, I
learned, in the course of the evening,
that they were a party of prospectors
sent out to the mountains in the Northern part of New Mexico and Arizona,
in the interest of a company of St. Louis
capitalists.

Boston Sunday Post (September 19, 1897).

GOLDEN MOUNTAIN
COCHISE & THE SECRET APACHE SOCIETY

ossibly linked to the theory that the Adams Diggings in Sno-Ta-Hay Canyon were only a prelude to an even larger gold deposit spoken of by Gotch Ear is the tale of the mythical "Golden Mountain" of Apacheria. After all, several accounts of the diggings had Gotch Ear specifically telling the miners that more gold could be found near a mountain close by. Some have taken this to mean that there was a huge placer within the mountain. Along these lines, in his Lost Adams Diggings pamphlet, W.H. Byerts wrote of an Adams hunter, called Captain Shaw, making a trip to Fort Wingate and visiting with an officer there about the Indians' knowledge of gold. The officer told Shaw that "the Indians often showed him specimens of ore that had come out of the malpais mountain to the south, stating that there was the largest vein of gold in that mountain that Indians or anyone else had ever found." In the same booklet, Byerts also noted,

> All of the big gold stories told by Indians, government scouts, old-timers and miners nearly point in the direction of the maplais mountain as the great gold mountain, and in early days it was called and is shown on some maps as 'Gold Mountain.'

The Byerts' pamphlet told of another expedition, possibly led by Gotch Ear, to the Golden Mountain. Byerts claimed, "A number of years [after the Adams story], a party of thirty Mexicans (claimed to be from Old Mexico) led by an Indian scout (possibly same one who led the Adams miners of the twenty-two men) headed for this same mountain." Unlike the disastrous fate that befell the Adams party, this expedition successfully mined the gold and got away with their lives. On top of that they were even said to return to get more.

Vintage postcard depicting the Malpais lava flow.

Though the area where it resided wasn't clear, I found a fascinating article dedicated to the legend of Apacheria's "Golden Mountain." The somewhat meandering article is difficult at times to follow, but it claimed the existence of a secret Masonic Apache brotherhood, the leader of which was buried on Golden Mountain. It appeared in several papers across the county in 1897, but this particular version was retrieved from the *Boston Sunday Post* of September 19, 1897:

A SINGULAR STORY.
THE APACHE CHIEF, COCHISE, AND HIS
FATHER—THE GOLDEN MOUNTAIN AND
THE SACRED LEGEND—MASONRY AMONG
THE APACHES.

In the Fall of 1870, writes a correspondent, while sitting on the porch of the hotel in Santa Fe, New Mexico, a party of twelve horsemen approached. Their horses were jaded and gaunt as from a long and difficult journey. The riders were dressed in buckskin overshirts, cavalry pants, heavy boots and large Mexican spurs. Dismounting at the hotel, the horses and men were cared for. A tall, slim, hickory-iron sort of a man, who seemed to be leader, made arrangements aside with the landlord. After supper, falling into conversation with the leader of the party, I learned, in the course of the evening, that they were a party of prospectors sent out to the mountains in the Northern part of New Mexico and Arizona, in the interest of a company of St. Louis capitalists.

The captain, as he proved to be, and so I shall hereafter call him, was an educated man, and a member of the company, and went on this perilous and toilsome expedition to satisfy a roving and restless disposition. They had gone beyond their intended limit at starting, and had penetrated into the edge of the Apache country. They had numerous fights with the Indians; but, being all old Indian fighters, had brought all their number back, though not without some ugly scars. At one time their whole number were taken prisoners by a midnight surprise and double their number of Apaches. They were held prisoners two days, and marched toward the Apache chief town, where they were to form the subject of a grand roast. But, the second night, they escaped by a stratagem, taking with them the leader of the Apache band, whom they afterward released on certain conditions. This leader is the bloodthirsty Apache chief, the chief who murders men, women and children.

The white party, before their escape, understanding something of their captors' language; unknown to them, learned, from a word let fall here and there, that the Indians had knowledge of some very rich mines, which the specimens that they had with them amply showed; but, from the desultory character of the remarks, could not learn the location of the treasure, and it was to this fact that the chief owed his life. This chief they spared when making their escape, at which time they sent the rest of the band to their long homes. They promised the chief his life and liberty if he would show them the "Golden Mountain," and tell them the "sacred legend of his fathers," which seemed to be in some way associated with the Golden Mountain. To this he finally assented, as the price of his life and liberty.

The riches of the Golden Mountain are even greater than the extravagant stories of the savages had led them to believe; but it is located in the heart of the Apache country, and utterly inaccessible till the Apaches are subdued. The guarding of this Gold Mountain, the keeping of the whites out of gold-fields of absolutely inestimable wealth, hoarded and piled up in the mountains of Arizona, is the first and greatest cause of the implacable hostility of the Apaches, even greater than the second cause—revenge. This chief showed them this wealth, guarded by the whole Apache nation, of which Capt.— [sic, name omitted] is prepared to take possession, with mills and mining apparatus, as soon as the Apaches are subdued. The chief gave them his legend, and they, as men of honor even to a captive, set him free.

"And the legend," says the captain, "it being late, I'll give you in the morning."

"So, here's to bed. Good night."

In the morning the captain and I walked apart on the outskirts of the town, to a grassy knoll, and sitting there he related to me the following strange, weird story.

A party of Apaches, while lying in ambush one day in the latter part of December, 1826, in Chihuahua, Mexico, on the Rio Grande, across the river from what is now the town of El Paso, Texas, watching a traveling cavalcade as it passed a clump of small trees, saw one of the number spring from his horse into the dense chapparal and disappear from the view of the horsemen. The cavalcade fired a few shots at on toward him and a half dozen of them dismounted and pursued in the direction he took, but of no avail. The escaping man ran directly toward where the Apaches lay in the bushes, and ran into their midst. They seized and bound him, mounted, and lashed him to a horse, and at once took flight. They traveled toward the Apache chief town by a circuitous and concealed route, and reached it after six days' travel.

The prisoner was much alarmed at first; but, finding that his death was not to be immediate, he seemed to put his mind to studying out some plan of escape; but they kept him securely bound till they arrived in camp. Then they decided to keep him until a grand fete day, some months ahead, and then put him through the gauntlet and end his life in a grand carnival. He for some time was as restless as a captive bear, walked up and down his small enclosure and talked to himself incessantly. But before the day arrived for his taking off—this is the captain's term, not the Indian's—he had become somewhat resigned to his captivity, had learned something of the Apache language, and gave them something of his history. They got interested in him, and promised to give him his life in return for his solemn promise that he would never attempt to escape. He married the chief's daughter, and, on the death of the chief, became chief himself. He had four sons and a daughter. The oldest son became chief himself, and is the chief who is the subject of our story.

The white chief taught them, while among them, the secrets of the Great Spirit, and these secrets have enabled them to make the Apaches the strongest tribe in the West; to pass through the country of the white man in safety everywhere; to obtain information of their enemies and their movements always, and from their very enemies themselves; and, by pass-words and signs, to know an enemy or a friend as far as seen. They always have kept and still keep one of their educated half-breeds in the camp of the whites, and, by the secrets of this great society, he is always able to keep them informed of every movement of any kind, and of every plan of attack on them, as soon as that plan is known to the chiefs of the enemy themselves. And, when captured, they are almost always sure to effect an escape, released by some member of the society among the enemy.

The great white chief told them that the society extended all over the world; taught them all the ceremonies connected with it; taught this maiden to make the badges and insignia worn by the initiated, and on certain days, the 24th day of June, and some others, they walked in procession, and held a grand dance at night. They believed him to be the son of the Great Spirit. He is buried at the Golden Mountain, and his grave is walled and covered with gold, and is their sacred place of worship. They gather now every year on the 24th of June.

This great white chief told them that he was "moons" (months) on his journey from his starting point; that he was taken prisoner in Batavia, N.Y., and from there taken to and confined in Fort Niagara, in the latter part of September of the same year in which he came to the Apache country. The reason of his imprisonment was on account of his going to publish a book divulging the secrets of the great society. He was kept prisoner at Fort Niagara till September 19th, when he was taken in a close carriage and driven, via Buffalo, N. Y., to Hennepin, Ill., on the Illinois river, and thence taken in a flat boat to the Mississippi river, down which he floated to New Orleans. There he was placed on a vessel and sailed to the mouth of the Rio Grande river, and proceeded up that river on horseback to El Paso, where the Apaches found him. His captors intended to give him into the hands of some Jesuit priests among the Indians, near where they captured him. His captors passed down through Mexico and escaped. That great white chief was the man supposed to have been murdered by the Masons, WILLIAM MORGAN, and the subject of this story, his son, COCHISE.

It's tough to say if this story was meant as satire or entertainment for the masses. Oddly enough, though, William Morgan was a real figure who disappeared under odd circumstances—but he most certainly was not the father of Cochise, who was born in 1805 before the Apache allegedly found Morgan. As for Morgan, he was born in 1774 and fought as a captain in the War of 1812. During time spent in Canada, Morgan

1829 illustration of William Morgan.

claimed to have ascended to the rank of a Master Mason. By the time he was in New York in the mid-1820s, he had become frustrated and disillusioned with his Masonic brethren, for he planned to publish an expose on them and their secret rituals called *Illustrations of Masonry*. Prior to its publication, Morgan was arrested on September 11, 1826, on a suspicious debtor's claim. Morgan's publisher saw to it that he was released, though he was subsequently rearrested. Under mysterious conditions, Morgan was let out of jail and transported to Fort Niagara just as the strange article in the *Boston Sunday Post* claimed.

What happened next has been lost to the annals of history, but stories circulated that Morgan was thrown overboard from a boat on the Niagara River, where he drowned. In October of 1827, a badly decomposed body was found on the shores of Lake Ontario and thought to be Morgan, though this was contested. Several Masons were later arrested and put on trial for his disappearance, and at least one source claimed that one of them confessed to the murder on their deathbed. In any case, Morgan's disappearance made his book a bestseller and even gave rise to an anti-masonic movement a bit later.

> ## MORE TALES OF APACHE MASONRY
>
> Oddly enough, I found a story that one could argue correlates with this one. The *Frontier Times* of October 1924 printed a story firsthand from an ex-Texas Ranger, W.R. Russell, who spoke of a band of Lipan Apaches who used Masonic distress symbols. The Lipans had killed some ox belonging to John Q. Daugherty near town of Leakey, Texas. Unlike the dubious article, which could have been simple yellow journalism for entertainment, this was a firsthand witness account. Russell said it occurred in early July of 1859. Specifically, when he and his fellow rangers caught up with the Lipan at the riverbank, this happened:
>
> > I was watching the water as well as other surroundings when all at once an Indian stepped upon the bank with a paunch of water in his hand, and at the same instant he discovered me. As I raised my rifle he exclaimed in a clear, loud voice, "Lipan Amigo!" and gave me the grand hailing sign of distress in Free Masonry in an intelligent manner. My rifle fired and he never gave any more signs. So you see the savage Indians, beyond a doubt, had Free Masonry among them, but at that time I did not know what that Indian meant by the sign he gave. [Rusell, W.C., "An Indian Gave Masonic Distress Sign," *Frontier Times* (October 1924) p.1]

Later, in June of 1881, a grave was discovered in a quarry two miles south of an Indian reservation in Pembroke, New York. Among the skeletal remains was a ring inscribed with the initials "W. M." As such, it was theorized the remains were Morgan's.

Despite this, strange stories of Morgan's survival persisted, such as the one published by the *Boston Sunday Post* in 1896.[1] While I certainly doubt there's any truth to Morgan becoming some kind of Apache war chief, I did find the mention of the "Golden Mountain" to be quite interesting. If nothing else, could it have been based upon the same "Gold Mountain" spoken of by W.H. Byerts related to the Lost Adams? Perhaps.

Chapter Notes

[1] Along those same lines were equally fantastic tales of Morgan becoming a pirate in the Cayman Islands where he was hanged.

10.

LAKE OF GOLD

EL DORADO IN THE ZUNI MOUNTAINS

Often confused with the Spanish-sought Seven Cities of Gold was El Dorado. While the seven cities were, as their name suggested, seven literal cities full of riches in the American Southwest, El Dorado was actually located in South America. It was also a man, as the name meant the *golden man*, referring to a king who covered his body in gold powder.[1] As part of a ritual offering, he would then submerge himself within a lake to wash off the gold dust. As such, the treasure sought by the conquistadors was not a city but the golden lake that the king bathed in.[2]

While neither El Dorado nor the Seven Cities of Gold were ever found, in Lost Adams Country did exist a place called Háwikuh. That was the village that Fray Marcos de Niza infamously identified as Cibola, the first of the Seven Cities of Gold, in the year 1539. The monk was too fearful to approach the wondrous city on his own and only gave a report of it in Mexico City when he returned. Instead, the task of exploring Cibola fell to Francisco Vasquez de Coronado in the spring of 1540. When Coronado arrived, he found not a city of gold and turquoise as promised, but a simple village of Zuni Indians not unlike the other pueblos he had come across. Fray Marcos de Niza was branded a liar, and had he not been a priest, it's possible the expedition would have stoned him.

A large party of citizens from Central City and Georgetown are now searching on the east side of the Mogollon range for the Adams diggings. Seldom a year has passed but what parties have left in search of these fabulously rich diggings. One or two of the parties, it is stated, have before visited the section of country for which the expedition is headed, and while the genuine Adams diggings, of which so much has been said and so little is really known, may not be in that particular part of the world, free gold in considerable quantity has been found there. The latest information of the Adams diggings comes from the Navajo country. The natives have found a lake from the bottom of which they bring up large chunks of free gold. The exact location of the lake cannot be ascertained.—Silver City Enterprise.

The *Clifton Clarion* of June 3, 1885.

However, interestingly enough, while the region boasted no seven cities of gold, it may have harbored something similar to the golden lake of El Dorado.[3] Tales of a rich, Cibola-like city residing on the shores of a lake in the land of the Zuni, which also happens to be in the land of the Lost Adams, were first alluded to by Adolph Bandelier in an 1892 article in *American Anthropologist*. Bandelier reported,

> Antonio de Espejo visited the Zunis and ... heard of a great lake on the shores of which were important settlements of sedentary Indians, all of which were rich in gold and precious stones. That lake was said to be at least several moons distant from Zunii. It is easy to recognize in those wild statements a distorted picture of the home of the Mexican Indians.[4]

The Coronado Expedition passing through New Mexico on the way to the Great Plains by Frederic Remington.

Before that, in 1885, the *Silver City Enterprise* had reported on a lake of gold in the same general region associated with the Navajo. It also linked the story to the Adams Diggings.

> A large party of citizens from Central City and Georgetown are now searching on the east side of the

Mogollon range for the Adams diggings. Seldom a year has passed but what parties have left in search of these fabulously rich diggings. One or two of the parties, it is stated, have before visited the section of country for which the expedition is headed, and while the genuine Adams diggings, of which so much has been said and so little is really known, may not be in that particular part of the world, free gold in considerable quantity has been found there. The latest information of the Adams diggings comes from the Navajo country. The natives have found a lake from the bottom of which they bring up large chunks of free gold. The exact location of the lake cannot be ascertained.

Zuni man at the ruins of Háwikuh, c.1900.

Unfortunately, further information on this golden lake in the country of the Navajo and the Zuni is difficult to find, so perhaps the *Silver City Enterprise* was simply spinning its own golden tale that day. In any case, this wasn't the only instance of the Lost Adams Diggings being associated with the Navajo and the Zuni, and more tales will be presented later.

Chapter Notes

---

[1] To be more specific, it would be *el hombre dorado.*
[2] The real location for this site is thought to be Lake Guatavita in Colombia.
[3] Because earlier in this tome I recorded tales of the Apache forging golden bullets, I did find one interesting old article that put forth the notion that the peoples of the Seven Cities of Gold also forged golden bullets—never mind that the Puebloans weren't using muskets or guns in the 16th century. The article, published in the *Oroville Weekly Butte Record* of October 10, 1863, stated that,

> ...for [Cortez] had heard the marvellous tale of the mysterious seven cities of Cibola, and the legends of an unknown people who dwelt in castellated towns and used bullets of gold and silver instead of lead; and our hunters were, therefore, actuated by much the same ambition which inspired the Spanish hidalgo, though more in a humble way,— but the city of Cibola or golden bullets saw not they...

[4] Bandelier, "'Montezuma' of the Pueblo Indians," *American Anthropologist* (Vol.5. October 1892). p321.

The tomb of Captain Cooney, seen above, located within the confines of the Gila Wilderness, six miles east of Alma, New Mexico.

11.

GOLDEN TOMB OF CAPTAIN COONEY

THE DEATH OF THE
FOUNDER OF MOGOLLON

The gold boom in the Mogollon mountain range of New Mexico is largely attributed to Captain James Cooney. The Canadian-born Cooney came to New Mexico after he volunteered to serve in the cavalry during the Civil War. Around the year 1870, Cooney was assigned to a mapping expedition when he was stationed at Fort Bayard. Cooney returned with sketches of water holes and trails as ordered. Not pictured on his charts was a ledge of gold ore he had found along Mineral Creek, though. He wisely decided to keep it a secret, unlike so many others who boasted of their finds in the first saloon within walking distance.

Cooney kept the secret of the gold ledge for years. After his enlistment expired in 1876, he returned to the region to begin prospecting. However, Cooney was driven off by Indian attacks and retreated to Silver City. Cooney returned to the Mogollons in 1878, this time with more prospectors to ensure safety in numbers along with professional equipment. With this, he successfully begat a little settlement, now deserted, called Clairmont near Copper Creek. His first big find was the Fanney Mine, and by 1878, Cooney had been instrumental in organizing the Mogollon Mining District. Born in its wake were the side-by-side towns of Mogollon and Alma, located eight miles apart.

In early 1880, Victorio's son-in-law, Torribeo, had been killed in a skirmish in the area. Naturally, the feared chief sought vengeance, which he achieved by attacking the Cooney mines and burning the outlying cabins. Cooney and his men sought refuge in the cabin of the Robert's family nearby as the Apache took possession of Alma. When the firing outside their cabin finally ceased, Cooney and another man, William Chick, went out to survey the area. Before departing, Cooney prophetically stated to the others that they would probably never be seen again.

While out, Cooney was hit in the thigh and fell from his horse in what is now known as Cooney Canyon. Cooney managed to take cover behind a tree and died fighting, as evidenced by the numerous spent rounds found nearby his bullet-ridden body. Cooney was later found sans his red-haired scalp, as the Apache had taken it as a trophy of one of their greatest foes. Upon the arrival of troops from Fort Bayard, the Apache fled, freeing Alma from their control.

Alma, New Mexico, estimated about the year 1900.

Cooney had been corresponding with his brother, Michael Cooney, who had also served as a captain in the army. Well aware of his brother's mining claims, Michael Cooney brought he and his family to the Mogollon region after his brother's death, arriving by the summer of 1880.

A few years later, Michael stumbled across an immense boulder near the spot where his brother had died. At once, he thought this could make for a worthy monument and mausoleum for his brother. Cooney had two of his most skilled miners go to work carving out a tomb inside of the boulder. Once finished, he disinterred his brother and had him "entombed in a rock of gold-bearing ore close to the site of the ambush," as author Michael Jenkinson put it in his article "Bonanza in the Mogollons."[1] After this, the entrance was permanently sealed and a cemetery was placed behind the stone mausoleum.[2] The boulder stands about ten feet high, atop which is a stone cross and a marble inscription at the sealed opening that reads, "J.C. Cooney, Killed by Victorio's Apaches, April 29, 1880, Aged 40 years."

As with anything of a sensational nature, Cooney's isolated tomb received conflicting measurements and descriptions from those adventurous enough to track it down. One of the first to write of the tomb was William French in 1884. He remembered in his book, *Recollections of a Western Ranchman*:

> This was a great cone-shaped boulder, that had fallen away from the main cliff and stood forty feet high, close by the road from Alma. It was twelve to fifteen feet wide at the base and tapered up to a point. In this, about ten feet from the ground, he had excavated a place for the coffin, closing it after the ceremony with a marble slab, with the name, age, cause of death, and the date. It was a monument to stay for all time.

In the *Albuquerque Tribune* of January 25, 1957, Jack Sadosuk wrote,

> Cooney's mausoleum is approximately 22 feet high and 15 feet wide and is made of adobe, rocks, brush and mud. It looks more like the entrance to a cave surrounded by thick brush than a mausoleum, and is the only landmark of the town which is now in total ruin.
>
> Both the Masonic Lodge and the Catholic Church contribute to the upkeep of the mausoleum. Dr. [E.R.]

Harrington said that Cooney's grave "remains one of the more romantic graves in New Mexico." Another reason Cooney's grave is kept "alive" stems from the fact that John Wayne has played Capt. Cooney in several western films.[3]

Cooney's Tomb, photographed by Harry Lucas sometime between 1882-1893.

True to his column's name, Howard Bryan visited the tomb for "Off the Beaten Path." In the *Albuquerque Tribune* of September 3, 1963, Bryan wrote,

> The dirt road leads east into the foothills of the towering Mogollons through a green and ever narrowing valley, passing a number of ranch houses and following closely along the banks of Mineral Creek.
> Near the point where the splashing waters of the small stream emerge from the deep and narrow Cooney Canyon, you come suddenly upon the huge boulder along the right or south side of the road, the road passing between the boulder and the stream.
> The boulder, which serves as a natural mausoleum, is about 10-feet high in the center and is surmounted by a stone cross. It is about 20 feet wide, and about 30 feet deep.

Apacheria Gold

The doorway of the unusual tomb is sealed with ore-bearing rocks, upon which a cross has been painted. A small iron fence with gate, painted silver, encloses a small plot directly in front of the rock tomb.

Naturally, the gravesite has been a staple of the region for many years now, with J. Frank Dobie writing of the marble inscribed tomb in *Apache Gold & Yaqui Silver*, prophetically stating, "A hundred years from now that mausoleum will no doubt still be the show place of the country."[4]

Chapter Notes

[1] *Frontier Times* (September 1971), p.15.

[2] Although some accounts glossed over this, Michael Cooney also had his son, John D. Cooney (b.1880, d.1891), buried there, as well as a grand nephew, Hugh Cooney (b.1896, d.1900).

[3] While I can't say for certain whether this statement has an inkling of truth to it, from my own admittedly brief inquiries into the subject of John Wayne playing Captain Cooney, I have yet to find the film in which this occurred.

[4] Dobie, *Apache Gold*, p.78.

APACHE KID IN FULL DRESS.

Anderson Daily Bulletin (January 16, 1897).

12.

GOLD OF THE APACHE KID
BEAR MOORE MURDERED!

The Apache Kid is probably one of the better-known outlaws of New Mexico. Among the pantheon of renegades called Kid, the Apache Kid probably trails just behind Billy the Kid and Butch Cassidy's partner in crime, the Sundance Kid, in notoriety. About the same age as Billy the Kid, Haskay-bay-nay-ntayl, alias the Apache Kid, was thought to have been born in the year 1860 and lived a similarly tragic life. Good-looking and well-liked for a time, the Apache Kid served as an Indian scout in 1881 and by 1882 was promoted to the rank of sergeant.

The Apache Kid's outlaw career began in 1887 when a skirmish occurred between several Indian scouts under his watch. In the altercation, the Kid's father was shot, and the Kid naturally retaliated along with others. This resulted in murder charges and a brief stay on Alcatraz Island until the Kid's conviction got overturned in 1888. However, a new warrant was issued for the Kid's arrest, and back to jail he went. During a transfer to Yuma Territorial Prison, the Kid and eight comrades overpowered their guards and escaped. Later dubbed the "Kelvin Grade Massacre," Sheriffs Glenn Reynolds and William A. Holmes were shot dead, while the stagecoach driver, Eugene Middleton, was also shot but survived.

The Apache Kid.

From that point forward, the Apache Kid was a fugitive and was often unjustly blamed for unsolved murders in the wilderness of Arizona and New Mexico. Various acts of thievery and rape were attributed to him, none of which could ever be proven. Because he was usually sighted within the range of the Lost Adams Diggings, the Apache Kid has more than a few ties to the Lost Adams gold.[1] For instance, the *News and Record* newspaper of March 20, 1939, vaguely made the claim that "They say that Apache Kid knew where the [Lost Adams] gold was and carried some of it away..."[2]

THE HIDING PLACE OF THE KID AND HIS BAND IN THE SAN RITA MOUNTAINS

Illustration from the *Philadelphia Times* of November 28, 1897, identifying the Santa Rita Mountains as the "hiding place of the [Apache] Kid and his band."

J. Frank Dobie tied up the Kid to the gold via the death of an old mountain man, Bear Moore, so named due to a face scarred from a grizzly attack. Legend had it that Bear Moore took to trapping and torturing bears thereafter, living in a secluded cave in the Gila Wilderness. Occasionally, he would wander into civilization with gold. His biggest find was a buckskin bag of flour gold he brought into Pinos Altos, for which he got $1,200.

Bear Moore was found dead near his cave by a fellow mountain man Nat Straw and an unnamed companion.[3] While many yarn spinners chose to speculate Moore had died fighting another grizzly, Dobie instead emphasized the gold found on his person via some speculations made by area resident Captain Micheal Cooney. Dobie said that Moore clutched a baking soda can to his chest that was found to be filled with "black sand mixed with flour gold and one big nugget."[4] Dobie added that, over the years, "Bear Moore must have buried at least one hundred thousand dollars of minted gold. Whatever he buried is still where he put it."[5]

Illustration from *The Southwesterner* of November 1, 1964, depicting Bear Moore in mortal combat with his enemy. Legend says that Bear Moore's ghost stalks the Gila Wilderness in search of more grizzlies to slaughter.

It had always been said that Moore was friends with the Apache Kid, who bought ammunition from Moore with gold. At the time of his death, a pair of rawhide horseshoes were found in his cave. And since Moore never used rawhide horseshoes, Dobie surmised that the gold must have been from the Apache Kid. Maybe it was even from the Lost Adams Diggings…

In the middle of these three Apache scouts is believed to be the Apache Kid, c.1880. It is thought that the Kid died sometime in the mid-1890s, but some old-timers claimed he was still alive and well and rustling cattle all the way into the 1930s.

Of course, in reality, Dobie probably just wanted to weave the colorful characters of the Apache Kid and Bear Moore into the Lost Adams lore for added interest to *Apache Gold & Yaqui Silver*. In the classic method of supposing, Dobie supposed that Captain Cooney supposed the following:

> Nevertheless, to Captain Cooney the gold that the Apache Kid presumably brought in to Bear Moore and the gold that Bear Moore most certainly possessed went further to prove that gold lay somewhere—somewhere where Adams wandered—waiting to be found.[6]

In any case, whether the Apache Kid ever possessed gold from Sno-Ta-Hay Canyon is unknown, he was for certain a staple of Lost Adams Country and Apacheria.

Chapter Notes

---

[1] As for another tie, Captain James Grey, who visited Sno-Ta-Hay Canyon a few times, claimed that he put a hit on the Kid and had him killed. J. Frank Dobie remarked he knew no less than four men who claimed to have been in on killing the Kid.

[2] It should be noted that this article mainly served as a review of *Apache Gold & Yaqui Silver* and was regurgitating information from the book as the author remembered it. Dobie didn't really make any such claim in the book, though.

[3] Old-timer Ben Kemp told a different story, that being that in 1912 an unnamed cowboy found Moore dead in his cabin rather than a cave.

[4] Dobie, *Apache Gold & Yaqui Silver*, p.91.

[5] Ibid.

[6] Ibid, p.93.

13

BLUE IRON DOOR MINE

W.H. BYERTS' MADE-UP MINE

One of the greatest proponents of the Adams story was Socorro-area mining engineer W.H. Byerts. As it was, J. Frank Dobie based the greater portion of *Apache Gold & Yaqui Silver* on Byerts' 1919 pamphlet entitled "The Adams Gold Diggings." In the early portion of the 20th century, New Mexico papers frequently reported either on Byerts' mining claims, his dry goods business, or his fruit orchard in the Socorro region. In the annals of history, though, Byerts is still remembered as one of Adams' chief prophets. Byerts, as it turned out, spun another golden fable before he latched onto the Lost Adams, though.

Enter the tale of the Iron Door Mine, said to have been lost during the Pueblo Revolt of 1680. As with the numerous "Padre Mines" of the Southwest, there are several other "Iron Door" mines, though this one was native to Socorro's Blue Canyon south of Socorro Peak. Under Spanish rule, Socorro was known as Holy Mission City—or so asserted Byerts. Though there was certainly a mission at Socorro at the time, as far as history goes, it was known as Nuestra Señora de Perpetuo Socorro, which was the first Catholic mission established in the area in 1626. According to the story of Byerts, the Iron Door Mine was begotten by area Jesuits, and it began operating in 1585, prior to the building of Nuestra Señora de Perpetuo Socorro.

BIG MINING DEAL IS
CLOSED AT SOCORRO.

Providence Mines & Reduction Company Disposes of Its Holdings. W. H. Byerts Is Purchaser.

Socorro, N. M., Jan. 17.—The Merritt mine out at the base of Socorro mountain has changed ownership again. W. H. Byerts this time being the purchaser from the Providence Mines & Developing company. The sale, made this week, included the mine and all appurtenances, including seevral adjoining claims, the buildings recently erected at the mine, and the old stamp mill in the south part of the city. The parties to the transaction decline to state the price of the property.

This property was bought last spring from A. D. Coon by the Providence company, the transaction being promoted by Dr. Henry Rolf Brown. Considerable money has since been expended in cleaning out the old mine, erecting buildings, and putting the stamp mill in condition to operate.

Mr. Byerts announces that he has already let a contract for a 1000 feet of development and that the work will be pushed with all possible speed. He says that he knows there is plenty of ore in the Merritt mine and that just as soon as he has made arrangements to handle the ore to the best advantage a mill will be erected to reduce or smelt it. If this enterprise is carried to a successful issue it will mean much to the business interests of Socorro.

El Paso Herald (January 17, 1912).

For nearly one hundred years, the mine produced until 1684—four years after the Spanish were expelled. (Obviously, Byerts only had a loose handle on the dates.) Byerts claimed that millions of dollars' worth of gold ore was mined and sent to Europe. What wasn't sent back to Spain was kept at the mines, where gold and silversmiths spent their days hammering the precious metals into jewelry. "A golden chandelier, suspended from the ceiling by heavy silver chains, together with fascinating altar ornaments of gold and silver, attested to the tremendous wealth of the Iron Door property," Byerts claimed. He also said that the mission there was "the wealthiest in the country at that time." As such, Holy Mission City then went on to become renowned across the Southwest.

Socorro's San Miguel Church as depicted by Confederate soldier Albert Peticolas on February 26, 1864, while passing through Socorro after the Battle of Valverde.

It all came to an end with a massive earthquake that struck in the year 1684—also the year of the Pueblo Revolt according to Byerts. Sounding like something out of a Cecil B. DeMille epic, Byerts said that "an earthquake of tremendous force broke off an overhanging ledge on Socorro Peak, flinging millions of tons of rock downward, completely burying the portal of the Iron Door Mine and trapping 500 miners." While the Spaniards worked hard to free the trapped miners, the Indians took advantage of the situation and revolted. The

Indians then drove every last Spaniard from New Spain and then proceeded to destroy all traces of the mine and Holy Mission City. Byerts wrote,

> Every vestige of this early civilization and immense wealth was wiped out; the church alone remaining, a monument to that which had gone before. All traces of the mines and city were destroyed during this time and not until the year 1880 was there another mining venture promoted.

W. H. Byerts, of Socorro, has a force of men at work on the Napoleon mine, which is one of the most promising lead propositions in the Caballo mountains.

Typical newspaper clipping of the time detailing Byerts' mining ventures. (*El Paso Herald*, March 13, 1900)

It's rather convenient for Byerts that the revolting Indians wiped away all traces of the once proud mission, considering no remains existed in Socorro of any such settlement as grand as Holy Mission City. At the time, Byerts' wild story worked, and he secured several new investors for his 1912 venture to bore for gold. In his article, Byerts reported that

> At this time a number of claims were located including the Torrence and Merrit, Morning Star and others. The Torrence and Merrit were worked from 1880 to 1885 and produced over a million dollars worth of bullion and the deepest workings did not go down over 150 feet, only the surface deposits being worked. All of these properties have been purchased by one company together with the location where the famous Iron Door property was located and are again known as the Iron Door Mines of Socorro. At the present time a tunnel is being driven under the old workings from the base of the mountain, which will open up the mine at a depth of

500 feet. The tunnel is now in over 500 feet and is being pushed day and night with every expectation of opening up one of the great gold-silver deposits of the southwest.

Socorro Peak as depicted on an old postcard.

However, a year later, the New Mexico Bureau of Mines reported in their No.8 Bulletin in 1913 that "Byerts Tunnel" was bored into Socorro Peak at a depth of 1,280 feet. It found nothing. In retrospect, in the *Frontier Times*, author Den Galbraith postulated that "W.H. Byerts willfully succumbed to a wild dream, which he pieced together from many sources— Indians, Mexicans, and all the old-timers he could talk to."[1] As Galbraith suggested, it was entirely possible that Byerts collected a hodgepodge of conflicting accounts, then, like Dobie and his version of the Adams Diggings, cobbled them into a romantic pastiche. Or, maybe it was entirely made up. As Galbraith put it,

Byerts left no documentation for his legend. Likely he got his story from the "archives" of some old-timer's mind, recapitulated around a campfire, aided and abetted by a jug of "Taos Lightning."[2]

Desert scene from Socorro County, New Mexico.

On a more objective note, Galbraith wondered if Byerts' tunnel of choice into Socorro Peak was merely the wrong one, and perhaps "Blue Canyon might well still hold a treasure guarded by the ghosts of 500 miners."[3] And it might.

To this author's surprise, and via the *El Defensor Chieftain* published out of the Socorro region, there does appear to be a real inspiration behind Byerts' Holy Mission City. According to area historian Paul Harden, Socorro was one of the first regions in the territory to have a lost treasure legend. In the early 1600s, it was recorded that Franciscan friars were indeed working with the Piro Indians to mine silver and gold from the area, presumably from Socorro Peak. According to Harden, the first church there was adorned with a great deal of silver, similar to Byerts' fantastic descriptions. It sported a silver communion rale, and it was said that even the twelve stations of the cross were made of silver.

Thankfully, a historical record of the riches exists via the journals of Fray Alonso Benavidez, compiled in 1629. Of the mission at Socorro, he recorded:

Well, all this land is full of great treasures - namely, very rich and prosperous silver and gold mines. As His affectionate chaplains and vassals, we customarily ask God for things like this....

"We give Him endless thanks for this in the name of Your Majesty - in particular for the range near the pueblo of Socorro, which is the principal and primary settlement of this province of the Piros....

"The ease with which silver may be taken from this range is the greatest in all the Indies. It would be wiser to extract eight ounces of silver here than many more ounces from other places, as elsewhere mining materials and supplies must be hauled from great distances to a source of water, which is certainly necessary to extract silver anywhere. But in these Socorro mines every thing needed for the job is right at hand."[4]

Depiction of forced Native American slave labor.

Somewhat similar to Byerts' account, it was the Pueblo Revolt of 1680 that brought about the mission's end. The Piro Indians did not take part in the revolt, however, and instead helped the friars carry away some of the valuables from the church, such as the silver stations of the cross. According to the legend, the padre in charge of the mission had the valuables of gold and silver buried nearby. Before departing for Mexico, he made a map to the buried treasure, which has now been lost.

"Somewhere around Socorro, and perhaps near the San Miguel mission, is buried treasure, a fortune estimated at $1 million or more today," Harden concluded.[5] With Harden being a reliable Socorro-area historian, perhaps Byerts' "made-up mine" had more truth to it than we were initially led to believe.

Chapter Notes

[1] Galbraith, "Iron Door Mine of Blue Canyon," *Frontier Times* (Sep/Oct 1964) p.41.
[2] Ibid, p.53.
[3] Ibid.
[4] Harden, "Buried Treasure," *El Defensor Chieftain* (March 2012), p.2.
[5] Ibid, p.3.

14.

DOC THORNE'S GOLD
ANOTHER LOST CANYON IN APACHERIA

The accounts of Adams and that of a man simply known as "Doc Thorne" have numerous similarities—mainly a gold canyon in Apacheria. Yet, for some reason, not many yarn-spinners or historians have ever tied the two together. While the "Doc Thorne Mine" might be too far east of the general location of the Lost Adams to properly connect the two, the similarities are there nonetheless. Like the Lost Adams, Doc Thorne's mine was located near some lava beds, in this case in the Four Peaks region of Arizona. Like Adams, Dr. Thorne seemed to have no first name and hailed from California. Dr. Thorne's story began in 1854 when he and seven other men left California for Louisiana. As their stage line traveled through Arizona, their coach was ambushed by the Pinal Apache near Maricopa Wells. The *Arizona Weekly Enterprise* of April 5, 1890, retold the story in grand fashion:

At the first shot the driver dropped the reins and fell forward, dead. The horses became frightened and in turning abruptly around, upset the ambulance; the front wheels became uncoupled and when Dr. Thorne, who was inside the wrecked vehicle, raised his head to look out, he saw some of the Indians making off with the horses.

DR. THORNE'S STORY.

HIS CAPTURE BY APACHES AND HIS FINAL ESCAPE.

His Life Saved by his Professional Skill---
Life Among the Indians---Discov-
ery of Gold—His Wanderings
and the Result of a Tis-
win Spree.

The true story of the capture of Dr.
Thorne by the Apache Indians and
his life while held a prisoner among
them has never appeared in print, and
indeed, the interest in his career
among the Indians has heretofore cen-
tered solely upon the wonderful discovery of gold it was reported that he had
made, to the exclusion of the details
of the circumstances that led up to
it.

Through the kindness of J. B. Hart,
who visited Dr. Thorne at his res-
idence at Casa Blanca three miles
above Socorro, New Mexico, in 1881,
THE ENTERPRISE is in possession of
the story as detailed by the doctor
only a year or two before he passed
away to his final rest.

Arizona Weekly Enterprise of April 5, 1890.

Illustration of wagon train at Maricopa Wells in 1857, where Dr. Thorne and his friends were allegedly ambushed.

The Indians took Dr. Thorne and one of his companions named Brown and started in a northerly direction, of the remaining members of the party he never learned their fate, but believed them to have been killed and it was probably the intention of the Indians to make their captives a sacrifice to their love of torture.

At their camp near the junction of the Black and White Rivers was a young Apache with a broken kneecap. Despite the efforts of the medicine man, it had become infected. The boy was so sick that his leg had to be amputated. Using chloroform to render the boy senseless, Thorne successfully amputated the knee.

To the Apache, it might as well have been magic, or what they more precisely called Power. Due to this act, Thorne was allowed to live amongst the tribe, while Brown mysteriously vanished—whether he escaped or was executed no one knows. Dr. Thorne treated the tribe's ailments regularly and particularly found himself in their good graces when he saved the life of their chief. As a reward, they told Thorne they would take him to a hidden canyon of gold since they knew it was of much value to the white man. However, Thorne would have to be blindfolded before he was taken there. Thorne felt as though his horse was led through a mountain range of some sort, and when the blindfold was loosed, he saw before him a canyon featuring a stream and a waterfall. Plus the promised gold, of course, which was in abundance. In their iteration of the story, the *Arizona Republic* of April 9, 1924, recorded the event thusly,

> The following morning [Thorne] was again blindfolded, and they crossed a mountain range requiring about two hours to reach the summit. After descending the far side of the mountain for about half an hour, they again traveled over rising ground a short distance, when they again descended into a valley, where the blindfold was removed. He was led to the bank of a small flowing stream and directly across the stream from where he stood a strong white quartz ledge cropped above the hillside. As he remembered afterward, this ledge of quartz was about three feet in thickness, and about in the center of it, for about four or five inches in width, was a vein of VIRGIN GOLD, apparently solid and unbroken.

After collecting several nuggets, Thorne was blindfolded again and led back to the Apache camp. A few months later, the chief allowed him to leave with his golden treasure. However, before he left, he was warned that he would be killed if he ever returned in search of the gold. Naturally, Dr. Thorne immediately organized a return expedition upon arriving in New Mexico. With his band of prospectors, he returned to the confluence of the White and Black Rivers. True to their word, the Apache attacked, killing many of the men and sending the rest off running. Dr. Thorne went on to New Orleans, still determined to return one day. There, Thorne raised funds for a second expedition. It, too, was foiled by the Apache. Thorne then interested his brother in a third trip. Again, the Apaches attacked, and only Thorne and one other man escaped. The third time was not the charm, and Thorne finally gave up his golden quest.

As with Adams, what was just recounted above was one of several different versions of the tale of Dr. Thorne. An alternate account, given in the *Arizona Weekly Enterprise* of April 5, 1890, stated that Dr. Thorne was never taken willingly by the Apache to see any gold. Instead, Dr. Thorne happened upon the gold purely by accident. The paper reported that Dr. Thorne often went hunting with a few Apache companions, and on one of their trips he stumbled across the gold by chance. The paper explained:

The doctor went out hunting almost every day with one of his companions and on one of these trips the boy picked up a nugget of gold from the bare bedrock in a wash west of some small, very red hills. At this place there might have been perhaps five thousand dollars in gold nuggets in sight. Dr. Thorne was so disgusted with the Indians that he didn't want to have anything more to do with them than was possible and he told the boy that it was of no account. The young Indian replied that it was good, and that the Indians could get powder and caps with nothing else. Dr. Thorne told him to throw it down; it was of no value, and walked away apparently unconcerned, but from that time forward he took close observations of the surrounding country in order that he might recognize the place again if he ever got free.

Chiricahua Apache Camp on Indian Reservation, Arizona Territory, 1886.

The *Weekly Enterprise* version of the tale took a fantastic turn that read like a pulp adventure novel. In it, Dr. Thorne miraculously escaped during a peace treaty gone wrong between the warring Navajo and Apache:

> After a long residence with these Indians the Apaches and Navajos had succeeded in making a treaty of peace between the two tribes, and the Indians with whom Dr. Thorne dwelt journeyed to the eastern side of the Mogollon mountains to participate in the grand ratification of the event and to complete its conditions. Navajos were to give the Apaches eight hundred sheep for the return of some of their squaws held in captivity, and to forever remain at peace. The meeting was a pleasant one and the exchange was fully completed when, to make the event more memorable a vast quantity of tiswin was brewed and the Indians all got drunk and began fighting. The Navajos succeeded in whipping the Apaches and took away the sheep they had just given them. In the confusion of the melee Dr. Thorne got among the Navajos and subsequently escaped to Cuvero, a little town out from Fort Wingate, and to civilization. He afterwards settled at Casa Blanco, near Socorro, where he married, raised a family of children and finally died in 1882 or 1883.

Similar to the other account, prior to his death, Dr. Thorne made repeat attempts to return to the gold. On the first, he suffered from snow-blindness in the Mogollon Mountains and had to be taken home, and the second time, into the White Mountains, his companions became skeptical and fed up with him and so returned.

Was there any truth to the tale of "Doc Thorne's Mine" considering the many different versions of the story? Colonel Jacob Snively, the famous gold-hound, apparently thought so. He went to Arizona in the fall of 1869 to hunt Doc Thorne's lost mine. Then there's the very similar tale of Surgeon Brayton, the soldier from Fort Yuma who was captured by the Tonto Apaches. During his confinement, he, too, found a canyon of gold somewhere in the vicinity of Weaver's Needle in Apacheria. Could it have been the same Apache canyon of gold found by Doc Thorne when he was detained by the Apache? Ultimately, like the Lost Adams Diggings, all that Doc Thorne's Mine has been able to produce is another fantastic story.

Unfortunately, no images exist of Mangas Coloradas, and above is shown his son and namesake, Mangus.

15.

MANGAS COLORADAS' GOLD
DID SNO-TA-HAY CANYON
COST HIM HIS HEAD?

There is a slight possibility that gold ingots from the Lost Adams Diggings played a part in the death of Mangas Coloradas, the great Apache chief, in the mining village of Pinos Altos. If Geronimo and Victorio were the terror of New Mexico Territory in the 1880s, Mangas was both their predecessor and their equivalent prior to the Civil War. Before the Mexican-American War of 1846-1848, Mangas reigned supreme in what is today southwestern New Mexico and, with his bands, often raided Mexican mining towns like Santa Rita. However, the great chief was more than happy to sign a peace treaty with the U.S. Army in the aftermath of the Mexican-American War. As the old saying went, the enemy of my enemy is my friend.

All was well between Mangas and his Apache until prospectors showed up in the Pinos Altos area and resumed mining as the Mexicans had done. So, in the early 1860s, Mangas came up with a plan. Rather than attacking the prospectors outright, he more or less planned to lure them into a trap via planted gold. Deception was often a ploy of the Apache according to John C. Cremony, a multi-lingual soldier who came to New Mexico at the onset of the Civil War and became one of the first recorded Anglos to learn the Apache language. Observing their ways, he explained the following in his 1868 book, *Life Among the Apaches*:

Deceit is regarded among [the Apache] with the same admiration we bestow upon one of the fine arts. To lull the suspicions of an enemy—and to them all other people are enemies—and then take advantage of his credence, is regarded as a splendid stroke of policy... When an Apache voluntarily discovers a rich mine to a white man, he is attempting to lay a trap for his destruction, baited by cupidity.[1]

John C. Cremony.

This method was used by Mangas when he came into the camp of a group of Pinos Altos prospectors and good-naturedly began chiding them on their recent strike. According to Mangas, their find was merely "poor diggings," and they would be old men by the time they had found enough gold to retire. Then, one by one, Mangas would approach different prospectors, telling them that he would take them to a rich gold vein not far away. As proof, Mangas would open up a little pouch on his person full of gold ingots. They had come from a stream outside of Apacheria, and the ingots were so plentiful one need not even pan for them, they could be plucked from the ground with ease. Cremony explained,

For a while each person so approached kept this offer to himself, but after a time they began to compare notes, and found that Mangas had made promises to each, under the ban of secrecy and the pretense of exclusive personal friendship. Those who at first believed the old rascal, at once comprehended that it was a trap set out to separate and sacrifice the bolder and leading men by gaining their confidence and killing them in detail, while their fates would remain unknown to those left behind.

The next time that Mangas came into camp, the miners drew their weapons and circled the chief, insisting on knowing what game he was playing. Some of the angrier men tied him to a tree and whipped him brutally. Cooler heads relented on their desire to kill Mangas, knowing full well it would start an Indian war—then they would have the Apache and the U.S. Cavalry alike after them for the death of Mangas. As such, they let him go. Mangas later returned with a vengeance, laying waste to the mining camp at Pinos Altos, ceasing nearly fifteen years of peace in the region. Or, at least that was the reason Cremony gave for the Apache uprising that occurred.

Prospecting camp in the Pinos Altos region.
(Taken from *The Pinos Altos Story* by Dorothy Watson)

"From [Cremony's] passages an embryo was born and subsequently took on a life of its own," wrote Mangas's biographer, Edwin R. Sweeney, in *Mangas Coloradas: Chief of the Chiricahua Apaches.* Sweeney continued that "This story, probably apocryphal, has become embedded as historical fact—a legend that writers and historians have perpetuated into this century."[2]

Whether Mangas was brutally whipped or not, the Apache under his command did begin attacking area prospectors, and Mangas himself was eventually killed and beheaded. It occurred in the summer months of 1862 after receiving a bullet wound to the chest that Mangas met with an intermediary to begin peace talks. To that end, in January of 1863, he conferred with the U.S. military officials at Fort McLane southeast of Silver City.[3]

Alleged image of Apache Tejo c.1894, the settlement closest to Fort McLane, where Mangas Coloradas conducted his fateful negotiations. As an aside, Apache Tejo is also where outlaw Billy the Kid joined up with a group of rustlers known as "the Boys" in 1877.

The precise details of what proceeded are murky, but it seems Mangas went to Fort McLane under the terms that he would be given provisions if he agreed to the peace treaty. Mangas made his negotiations with the officers in command and was then taken away to a holding area for the night. From the best that researchers today can tell, a plan was afoot to kill Mangas from the get-go. The soldiers in charge of Mangas were given secret orders to "entice" him to escape. They did so by tying Mangas to the ground and branding him with their fire-heated bayonets. Mangas was untied, and when he naturally began to flee, this gave the soldiers grounds to shoot him as he was "escaping."

Mangas met with Brigadier General Joseph R. West, pictured above when he later served as a Louisiana senator from 1871 to 1877. In 1862, he was a commanding officer of the California militia. West supposedly told the sentries set to guard Mangas Coloradas, "Men, that old murderer has got away from every soldier command and has left a trail of blood for 500 miles on the old stage line. I want him dead tomorrow morning. Do you understand? I want him dead."

Like his contemporary, Geronimo, it is said that Mangas Coloradas's skull was removed from his corpse. So the story went, the soldiers were amazed by Mangas's unusual height for an Apache, standing six foot six inches tall, and decided to behead him, then boil the severed head to get the skull. Somehow, the skull ended up in the possession of New York phrenologist Orson Squire Fowler. Unlike urban legends, such as tales that Geronimo's skull was stolen from his grave in 1918, sketches of Coloradas' skull appeared in Fowler's 1873 book *Human Science* on page 1196.

Orson Squire Fowler.

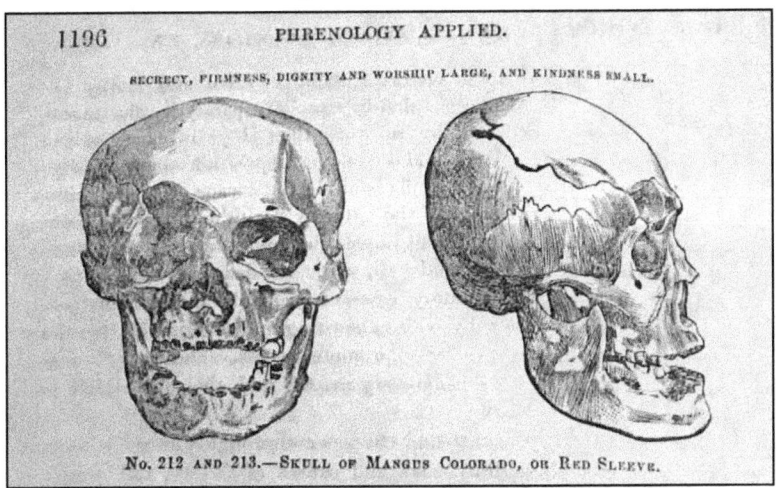

Drawing of the skull of Mangas Coloradas from *Human Science*.

The Apache were naturally enraged by this act of desecration and feared that Mangas Coloradas could not properly roam the "Happy Place" in the afterlife without his head. Ace Daklugie, son of the Apache chief Juh, told historian Eve Ball of Mangas' death and mutilation, explaining that at first the soldiers simply threw the great chief into a shallow ditch outside of camp. Daklugie continued,

> That was not the worst: the next day they dug up his body, cut off his head, and boiled his head in a big black kettle. To an Apache the mutilation of the body is much worse than death, because the body must go through eternity in the mutilated condition. Little did White Eyes know what they were starting when they mutilated Mangas Coloradas.[4]

To return to the question of whether or not the incident at Pinos Altos between Mangas and the miners related to the Lost Adams gold or not, Daklugie told Ball, "Mangas Coloradas could have shown them plenty of gold. All the chiefs know where it is."[5] Some have linked this statement to the Lost Adams, thinking that the gold in Mangas' pouch came from Sno-Ta-Hay Canyon, but, frankly, in Apacheria, it could have come from anywhere.

Chapter Notes

---

[1] Cremony, *Life Among the Apaches*, p.287.

[2] Sweeney, *Mangas Coloradas*, p.400.

[3] Formerly Fort Wheeler, the fort was short-lived, existing between 1860-1864.

[4] Ball, *Indeh*, p.20. In a later interview, Daklugie told Ball that the skull had been sent to the Smithsonian, a point still debated among scholars to this day.

[5] Robinson, *Apache Voices*, p.111.

16.

DUTCHMAN'S GOLD
THE TALES OF SNIVELY & SCHAEFER

Dutchmen seem to have a strange affinity for lost gold in treasure tales. As recorded earlier, one of the other lone survivors of the Adams party was a man simply referred to as "the Dutchman." As such, from time to time, the Lost Adams Diggings was occasionally called the Lost Dutchman's diggings, gold, mine, canyon—fill in the blank. Greatly confusing this was a more famous treasure further west, that of Arizona's Lost Dutchman Mine found by Jacob Waltz somewhere in the Superstition Mountains east of Phoenix.

The "Dutchman" of the Adams party is a bit harder to identify, but the most devoted researchers of the Lost Adams Diggings think there's a strong possibility that he was Colonel Jacob Snively, born around 1809. Unlike some of the shadowy figures that drift in and out of treasure tales, Snively left quite a wake in the annals of Western history. When he first came to the West from Pennsylvania, Snively acted as a surveyor for the Republic of Mexico in 1835. Later, he was a military officer for the Republic of Texas. While Colonel Snively's military career was long and distinguished, even stretching into the Civil War for the Confederate Army, it was Snively's mining ventures that drew the most attention historically speaking.

In 1858, he came to New Mexico Territory and discovered gold placers on the Gila River about twenty miles east of Fort Yuma. This, in turn, created the gold boomtown of Gila City, Arizona, which has long since been a ghost town. Next, Snively discovered a huge silver streak in the Castle Dome Mountains north of Gila City. As if that wasn't enough, in the mid-1860s, Snively had found a mystery gold mine somewhere in the Datil Mountains somewhere west of Socorro. In a narrow box canyon where the strike occurred, Snively built a cabin and a sluice box to mine his gold. To keep suspicions at bay, he didn't sell his gold in the same towns and alternated between Pinos Altos, Socorro, and Silver City. Though his box canyon with a cabin sounded the same as the Lost Adams Diggings, Snively never spoke of being part of a group of prospectors who were massacred by the Apache under Chief Nana. As such, some have wondered if Snively purposefully and wisely removed himself from the tale of Adams, or if perhaps he found a similar canyon or the same canyon apart from the Adams group.

Postcard of Tres Hermanas Mountains near Deming.

In any case, by 1870, Snively was driven away from the area by Warm Springs Apache. Actually, it was the Apache that eventually spelled the old gold-hound's doom. Snively was fresh off a rich strike again at White Pine, Nevada, in 1869 before returning to Arizona, where some say he hunted Doc Thorne's lost gold. Snively met his death while hunting a silver ledge in the Bradshaw Mountains in the early spring of 1871.

Jack Swilling with his Apache ward Guillermo Swilling, c. 1875.
(Arizona State Library, Archives and Public Records)

Snively had set out with a group of prospectors from Phoenix in the direction of Wickenburg when he and his party were attacked by what some estimated to be 150 Apache at the White Picacho. Snively was shot by arrows, causing him to fall into an arroyo, where he was left behind by his fellow prospectors who managed to escape. His badly decomposed corpse was found partially devoured later and was hastily buried. The roving Apache finally got the old Indian fighter after many years of evading death at their hands.

Snively had a successor of sorts named Jake Schaefer, also a "Dutchman," who may have found Snively's old mine. In the year 1872, Schaeffer was hired as a cook for a group of soldiers patrolling the Deming region along the Mimbres River. On a hunting excursion, Schaeffer became separated from the main group. He turned up many days later at Fort Craig near Socorro, having wandered hundreds of miles. He was stark naked and out of his mind. All that he carried was a sack of gold nuggets weighing nearly ten pounds. (He was said to later cash them in for $3,000, though, as usual, accounts vary.) Later, as his sanity slowly returned, he couldn't remember where he had found the gold, only that he had passed a mysterious mountain with the face of a woman painted on it. Like Adams, Schaeffer spent the rest of his days trying and failing to retrace his steps. In 1874, his tenure in New Mexico came to an end and he gave up on the gold and returned to Virginia. Before departing, he left instructions to the gold to friends: "Ride north along the Datil Mountains, across the Plains of Agustin, until you see the Magdalena Mountain. Then, due north into the mountains. There you will find a very narrow box canyon. You will have to dismount from your horse to enter it." So far as anyone knows, the only other soldier to find the canyon was an unnamed Buffalo Soldier who made two trips to the canyon, getting a little gold before the Apache could catch him.

Seven years later, Snively's friend, Jack Swilling, retrieved Snively's remains and had him reburied in the Swilling family cemetery. The duo had been friends ever since Swilling met Snively at the Gila City placers and followed him to Pinos Altos.

Of his friend, Swilling said, "His sad fate has cast a gloom over our settlement. He never made an enemy, but always friends. He was the prince of gentlemen and the pink of chivalry."

17.

NAVAJO & ZUNI GOLD
R.C. PATTERSON'S QUEST

L ike all unfound treasures, the Lost Adams Diggings has been waiting to be found in many diverse locations over the years. In the late 1880s and throughout the 1890s, the diggings had moved from the confines of Apacheria to those of Dinétah—the homeland of the Navajo.[1] Perhaps because Apacheria had failed to yield the Adams Diggings, papers began placing the lost gold on the Navajo Reservation within northwestern New Mexico, and some accounts even replaced the Apache with the Navajo when it came to who killed the Adams party.[2] *The Socorro Chieftain* of January 9, 1904, for instance, put forth the strange notion that Adams had paid the Navajo to work the diggings. It stated,

> Adams had made arrangements with the Navajos to allow him to work the diggings and he paid them liberally for the privilege. He came into Fort Wingate with a large amount of gold to deposit, and started in a northeasterly direction for the diggings with a more complete outfit. When he had departed the excitement consequent upon the display of so much gold induced the forming of another party to follow him, and the Navajos, fearing a general invasion, killed the entire party.

ADAMS LOST MINE IS "DISCOVERED" BY NAVAJO

[Special Dispatch to the Morning Journal.]

Cold Springs, N. M., May 24.—A Navajo Indian who is well known in McKinley and Valencia counties, came through Cold Springs today with specimens of seemingly rich gold ore, which he claims came from the old diggings known as "Adams' Lost Mine," about four days' ride from here. The Indian is not only confident that he has found the lost mine, but is willing to divulge the secret to an old-time friend, August Houser, a New Mexican pioneer. The latter has confidence in the Indian and the two are now outfitting for an expedition to the reported gold strike, which if verified will relieve many a burdened prospector of the faint hope that he has discovered the coveted diggings.

The *Albuquerque Morning Journal* of May 25, 1912, reported more tales of the Adams Diggings on Navajo land.

Lost Adams Diggings or not, the Navajo Reservation certainly contained tales of gold and talk of hidden riches popped up from time to time. "The Navajo Indians who … range over the Datil country, seem to know where there is a placer where large gold nuggets are to be found," the *Albuquerque Citizen* reported in 1908. It continued that one Navajo had been seen with "chunks of gold as large as the joint of a finger."[3]

Apacheria Gold

An article in the *Albuquerque Morning Journal* of May 25, 1912, reported that a Navajo man had come into Cold Springs with "specimens of seemingly rich gold ore" that he claimed came from the Adams Diggings and was four days away by horse. Not too far from Cold Springs was Tinaja Canyon, which was exactly where an old Federal Writer's Project report situated the Lost Adams Diggings. In that case, Adams was named Adam, and had a lone partner that he worked his mine with.

Zuni Mountains of New Mexico c.1908.

"The Story of Adam's Diggings" by L. Raines claimed that "Many years before New Mexico became a state, Adam and his partner worked a mine in the Zuni Mountains." More specifically, it claimed the find was near Tinaja Canyon. J. Frank Dobie also covered the possibility of the diggings being located on Zuni Land in *Apache Gold & Yaqui Silver*:

In 1929 a woman in Flint, Michigan, who claims to be a grandniece of Davidson [a survivor of the Adams party], wrote that he died soon after escaping from the diggings, leaving a diary and a map that located the gold in the Zuñi Indian reservation. Some men in Utah had an option on the map, however; their use of it by scouring over the Zuñi country in an airplane did not prove anything.[4]

Dobie also reported on a character called "Sixshooter Charlie" in *Apache Gold & Yaqui Silver*, who was sure the Adams gold was located on a Navajo Reservation. Charlie claimed that he had "positive evidence that Adams' supply party had come in from that direction to the place now called Gallup."[5] Old-timer Washie Jones placed the diggings on either a Navajo or a Zuni reservation as well in *Cow Dust and Saddle Leather* by Ben Kemp and J.C. Dykes.

Among the more credible people connected with Adams to believe the gold was on the Navajo reservation was R.C. Patterson. As it was, Patterson met Adams in 1876 at Horse Springs, and afterward helped him search for his lost gold.[6] Patterson's time with Adams apparently led him to believe that the diggings were north of Gallup somewhere in the Navajo Reservation, as evidenced by the fact that Patterson mounted an excursion into the region in 1888. Using his commission as a deputy sheriff, Patterson and his men entered the reservation under the pretext of looking for stolen horses.

George Ross, one of the men with Colonel Patterson in his search for the lost Adams diggings, while out in the Zuni Mountains, where he stopped to cook a meal, was, it is believed, fatally wounded by the Zunis. He reached Gallup, N. M., Tuesday it is believed in a dying condition.

This blurb alluded to yet another Lost Adams expedition headed by R.C. Patterson and also another fatality along the way. (*Lyon County Times*, May 3, 1890)

According to George E. Christilaw, a part of the expedition, they set out on September 8, 1888, from Socorro before heading to Gallup where the newspapers picked up their trail. Nine of their number decided to give up on the trip midway through, but a few of them, including the narrator and Patterson, worked the canyons along the San Juan River.[7] No gold was found, and at least one of their party was killed by the

Navajo.[8] Actually, for a time, even Patterson was believed dead until he returned to civilization alive and well, but sans the gold.

> R. C. Patterson was a business visitor in Socorro last Saturday. He said that he had just returned from the Navajo ccuntry, where he went in search of the Patterson diggin's, not the Adams diggin's this time, but that the heavy snow up there drove him out. Mr. Patterson still looks hale and hearty, as though he might still be good for many years of hardship, if need be, that would appall many a man much younger.

Interestingly, a newspaper blurb not long after implied that Patterson did not actually consider this a hunt for the Lost Adams Diggings, but an entirely different gold vein:

> R. C. Patterson was a business visitor in Socorro last Saturday. He said that he had just returned from the Navajo country, where he went in search of the Patterson diggin's, not the Adams diggin's this time, but that the heavy snow up there drove him out. Mr. Patterson still looks hale and hearty, as though he might still be good for many years of hardship, if need be, that would appall many a man much younger.[9]

The next year in 1889, a party allegedly led by Adams himself endeavored to do the same, although the results of their expedition is unknown since newspapers only reported on its beginning and not its end.[10] In any case, it's highly likely that the expeditions of Patterson and "Adams" at the close of the 1880s inspired a more fruitful prospecting trip in the winter of 1890—one that would become highly sensationalized...

Chapter Notes

---

[1] Dobie, *Apache Gold & Yaqui Silver*, p.99.

[2] As to further possibilities that it was actually the Navajo rather than the Apache that massacred the camp, Jack Purcell pointed out in his *Lost Adams Diggings* that in the Byerts' version of the tale, the prospectors were beheaded and their heads placed atop poles that the Indians danced around. Purcell noted in the footnote, "At least one searcher argues this passage is evidence the massacre was done by Navajo tribesmen, instead of Apaches. Navajo depredations frequently involved taking heads. Many accounts exist describing this behavior."

[3] *Albuquerque Citizen* (October 31, 1908).

[4] Dobie, *Apache Gold & Yaqui Silver*, pp.27-28.

[5] Ibid, p.99.

[6] Patterson was actually one of the very first sources of the legend, and his brief account of it was published in the *Socorro Chieftain* in 1897. I didn't summarize it in *Legend & Lore of the Lost Adams* because it didn't include anything worth noting that contradicted Dobie's version.

[7] An article published years later in the *Albuquerque Weekly Citizen* of January 27, 1900, implied that R.C. Patterson was the leader of the 1890 party that was arrested by the soldiers covered in Chapter 22 of this book. It should be noted that this is certainly a mix-up, as Patterson was never noted in any of the firsthand accounts of the 1890 party.

[8] Government reports of the time confirmed the death of a man by the last name of Swift in the party.

[9] Invariably I find interesting articles, clip them, then either lose or forget to save the source. This is one such instance.

[10] See Chapter 17: "Adams Rides Again," in *Legend & Lore of the Lost Adams*.

18.

PHANTOM MOUNTAIN
THE GOLD'S HAIRY GUARDIAN

Frontier Times undoubtedly published some strange pioneer stories from time to time. Among the strangest of them all was one concerning a phantom mountain of gold guarded by a hairy wild man. "The Mountain That Disappeared" by Frank Mason told the tale of two prospectors and a beautiful Indian maiden's voyage through a particularly strange part of Apacheria.

The story came courtesy of John Hix, who arrived in Arizona from Missouri in 1871 and wrote a diary recording the adventure to follow. For a time, the young man worked at prospecting in the area around Tucson before joining up with a seasoned prospector by the name of Lemuel "Jackass" Dodson. The two were opposites, as Hix was young and short-statured, while Dodson was a tall old-timer. Dodson suggested prospecting an area forty miles from Flagstaff called the San Francisco Wash, today located in the confines of the Navajo Reservation. From there, they traveled to Canyon Diablo, in the vicinity of which was a tribe of Indians that Hix unfortunately didn't identify, but presumably they were Navajo. Dodson was sweet on an Indian maiden there named Shining Flower, and he took her with them on the trip to act as their guide. They were headed for a mountain near which gold nuggets could be found, some as large as a man's thumb.

Upon arrival, Hix found a nugget nearly the size of the palm of his hand near the top of the mountain. And elsewhere, in a spot he neglected to record in his diary, he found seventeen additional nuggets. The next day, he and Dodson climbed to the top of the peak but found no gold vein. Suddenly, down below, they heard Shining Flower scream. The men raced down the summit back to camp, where they found Shining Flower hysterical. She claimed to have seen a hairy Wildman:

> She said she had seen something in the desert which she had thought to be a man, and that later she saw it again near camp. "He had long whiskers and hair down his back," she said in describing the intruder. "When he saw that I was looking at him, he turned and ran into the brush."[1]

The men brushed off her worries as Indian superstition and went back to searching for gold on the mountain. Considering there was next to no water in the area of the mountain, they felt that no wildman could survive in the region. Therefore, Shining Flower must have simply been seeing things they surmised. However, that night at camp, all three of them heard a "strange and mournful sound from the hillside above camp."[2] At first they thought it might be a wolf, but it wasn't. Nor did they think it was a panther. Whatever it was, it was unlike anything either of them had heard before.

The next day, Shining Flower was too frightened to remain at camp and accompanied the men to the top of the mountain. Though they again found much gold in the form of nuggets, they could find no placer vein to source it from. Therefore, Dodson concluded that the main vein may have been destroyed in an earthquake that scattered the gold and shrunk the mountain from its original size.

When they returned to camp, they found it unmolested. Dodson chided Shining Flower that there had obviously been nothing to worry about. That night, the strange noises resumed, though. Shining Flower voiced the opinion that it was an evil spirit, which Dodson brushed off as superstition, stating it must be an animal with a wounded throat, hence the unfamiliar sound. Again, he claimed that no human could make a cry like that.

Ominously, the next morning, their pack animals were nowhere to be found. Neither were their water bags. Something had absconded with them. Dodson took the only rifle in the group and followed the burro tracks, determined to get them back, while Hix and Shining Flower stayed at camp. Eight days later, Dodson failed to return. Hix and Shining Flower set out across the dry desert sans any water. Though they tried to take some gold with them, eventually, it became too much of a burden, so they cached it under a rock.

Shining Flower became too weak to walk, and likewise, Hix was too weak to carry her. They agreed he would search out a water source and return to her. After a few days wandering, Hix came upon the watering hole at which he and Dodson had earlier filled their skin containers. With nothing to transport any water with back to Shining Flower, Hix had no choice but to venture on to the Indian village from which she had came. There, the tribe was receptive to Hix, and agreed to help him rescue Shining Flower, assuming she was still alive. Dodson certainly wasn't. On the trail they found him dead with two bullet holes in his back. Had the mysterious wild man shot him? Or had it been someone else?

Stranger still, though Hix and the Indians trailed the burro tracks southwards towards the mountain, the mountain itself failed to yield itself on the horizon. On his journey, Hix recognized two distinct landmarks. One was a ravine through which they had passed, and another was a lone tree on which he had hung their water bags for a time. Otherwise, the landscape seemed completely different. Blake wrote that to Hix the country had become unrecognizable:

> Every landmark was gone except the tree on which he had hung the water bags. Where ravines had been before, the ground was level as a table. The whole thing was more than bewildering—it was awesome—and Hix had no stomach to explore further.[3]

Neither the large golden mountain, said to be a thousand feet high, nor Shining Flower, were ever seen again. Later a sheriff theorized that an Indian half-breed was to blame for the strange man seen outside of the camp, even though he failed to match the description of the hairy wildman seen by Shining Flower. Furthermore, the sheriff's suspect could prove he had been herding cattle at the time of the incident. (If anything, it seemed as though the sheriff just had it in for the man and was trying to pin the murder on him.)

The depiction on Tulare County, California's Painted Rock is thought by many to represent a Sasquatch. (Garrick Mallery, *Picture-Writing of the American Indian*, in the *10th Annual Report of the Bureau of Ethnology to the Secretary of the Smithsonian Institution*, 1888-'89, by J. W. Powell)

Mason admitted that it strained credibility when he first heard the account, most notably the fact that something as big as a mountain could disappear. As speculation, Mason wondered if an earthquake may have caused it:

Could a mountain disappear? I don't know—but it is true that there was a shifting of the Indians in that area to the north in 1872. They told of great rumblings that shook the earth and drove them to other lands. If such an upheaval occurred, then that is the clue to another lost treasure.[4]

And, as for one final, lingering question: could the wild man have been a Sasquatch? As it was, the Navajo and other Native American tribes had many legends of hairy giants in the wild. An article from the *Albuquerque Evening Herald* of February 3, 1913, reported how, on the Navajo Reservation near Gallup, a young Navajo man had killed a hairy wild man there. Perhaps not coincidentally, the hairy wild man had been seen in the vicinity of a gold mine on the reservation. Is there a heretofore unknown tie between Sasquatch and gold? Who knows, but it certainly made for an entertaining story.

Chapter Notes

[1] Mason, "The Mountain That Disappeared," *Frontier Times* (June/July 1963), p.35.
[2] Ibid.
[3] Ibid, p.67.
[4] Ibid.

AN IMMENSE WILD MAN KILLED IN THE HILLS.

Albuquerque Evening Herald - February 3, 1913 - New Mexico Hideous Monster Is Reported Slain Near Navajo Mine; News Brought to Gallup by Albuquerque Man.

Gallup, N.M., Feb. 3. - A vicious, grotesque, and hideous looking wild man was killed in the hills back of Navajo mine last Saturday morning by a young Indian boy. The object, beast or man which ever it may be termed had been menacing the natives in their daily work for the past five months. The man was entirely without clothing, his entire body being covered with a coat of thick, coarse dark hair four inches long. The only part of him which was normally human was his feet, which would perhaps have required a No. 10 or 11 shoe. The face was chinless and only one lip was visible; the forehead sloped directly backward of the head, something after the fashion of the Pin Headed Cannibal. Small beadlike pink eyes were concealed, set deep in the sockets behind long and grimy eyelashes. The arms of the man were four feet long, and long sharp cat-claws adorned the finger tips. The man measured full seven feet in height.

For five months the natives had been telling of this menacing object which had been seen by hundreds, prowling about the rocks both day and night, and it would always make a rapid escape over the rocks and disappear in a certain canyon, traveling with great speed. A young Indian boy was traveling across the country with a Winchester, and evidently must have cut the monster off from his retreat. He came straight towards the boy who raised his rifle and fired twelve shots at his body, eight of which took effect, but only one of them did any serious damage. The body was taken into camp at Navajo and the company physician prepared a glass coffin in which the body will be preserved in alcohol.

The Gallup Independent after telling this tale explains it as follows:

D.T. Brown, an itinerant photographer from Albuquerque brought the story back from a trip to the mines Sunday. What had the man been drinking, or what ailed him we are unable to say.

19.

GERONIMO'S GOLD
A NEBULOUS TREASURE CACHE

Traditonaly, Chief Nana was the Apache in charge of the group that massacred the Adams party at Sno-Ta-Hay Canyon, but occasionally, some storytellers replaced Nana with Geronimo. While Geronimo most certainly wasn't responsible for massacring the miners, Geronimo was thought to have his own gold cache located somewhere either in Arizona, New Mexico, Texas, or maybe even Mexico—the list was long and distinguished. Some thought the mysterious gold source was Sno-Ta-Hay Canyon, though.

Generally, the story went that while he was interred at Fort Sill, Oklahoma, Geronimo made friends with either one of the soldiers or one of the traders there. Geronimo told the man that if he were to free him, he would take him to a rich gold mine. However, while Geronimo was allowed to travel for the sake of fairs and publicity events, otherwise he was not let off the reservation, especially not for a prospecting trip that may well turn out to be an ambush. Considering the vagueness of Geronimo's promise, the location of his fabled gold mine has spanned the entirety of the Southwest to a degree. Most agree that it is in Arizona, either in the Verde River area or in the Superstition Mountains in a place called Geronimo's Cave. Others placed it in New Mexico in various locations, and yet others in the Guadalupe Mountains of Texas.

Leland Lovelace explained in *Lost Mines and Hidden Treasure* that, "There is plenty of proof that Geronimo knew a source of gold, for he sometimes used it as a medium of exchange. He much preferred, however, to take by trickery or by right of conquest, when not able to cajole or prevail by chicane."[1]

Essentially, different authors liked to attribute Geronimo's remarks to whatever location suited the story they were telling. J. Frank Dobie linked it up with both the malpais version of the Adams Diggings and also a separate treasure in the Guadalupe Mountains. Similarly, Leland Lovelace connected

Geronimo's gold with that of the mysterious canyon allegedly found by Dr. Thorne in *Lost Mines and Hidden Treasure*. John D. Mitchell in *Lost Mines of the Great Southwest* identified the location as that of the Verde River region of Arizona. And Mitchell's version might be the right one considering he was one of the lone sources to give Geronimo's informant the name of Will James, identified as a translator at Fort Sill. W.C. Jameson took the Verde River location in greater detail and ran with it in his book *Lost Mines and Buried Treasures of Arizona*. In it, he explained the origins of Geronimo's gold.

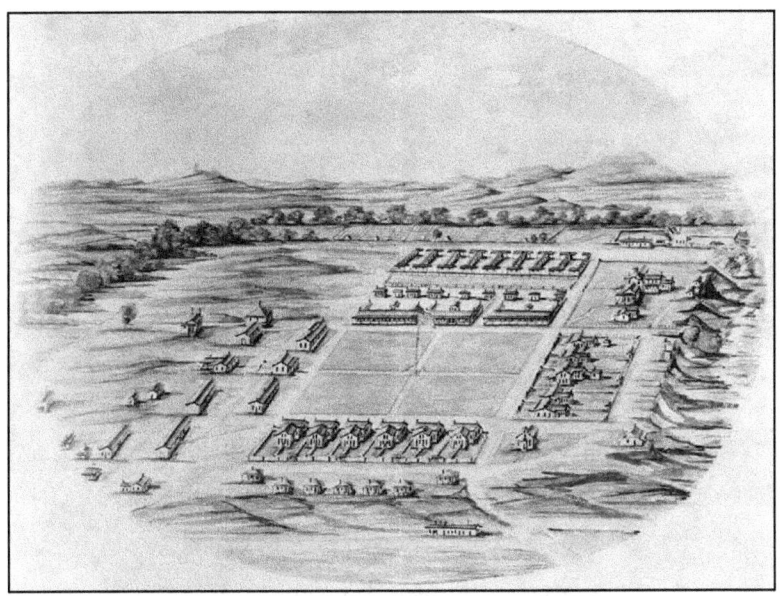

Illustration of Fort Sill, Oklahoma, c.1800s.

Jameson's origin story for Geronimo's gold began during the Spanish occupation of the Southwest and had a group of Jesuits befriending a group of Apache in the Verde River country. After bestowing the Apache with gifts, supposedly the Apache led the Jesuits to a small canyon along the Verde River. Immediately, the Jesuits chained the Apache together and made slaves of them, forcing them to mine the gold. As the Apache were forced to dig into the earth, the gold vein became larger and richer the deeper they went. Over the years, the other Apache in the area would attempt to free their enslaved brethren. Over time, due to the attacks, only six Spaniards remained alive. The survivors decided it was best to pack up as much gold as they could and flee, and so they did. The Apache attacked once again, however, until only two men remained. The duo retreated back to the canyon, hid their gold in a cave, and fled southwards towards Mexico. Although they planned to return later in greater numbers, they never did.

Geronimo, center, and seven other Apache men, women and a boy posed in front of tents at the Louisiana Purchase Exposition, St. Louis, c.1904.

Several years later, it was said Geronimo discovered the old mine. Using the previously mined gold—don't forget, Apaches weren't forbidden from picking up gold, but they were forbidden to dig it themselves from the earth—Geronimo would periodically take ingots with which to purchase rifles and ammunition. Supposedly, Geronimo swore his men to secrecy on the location of the mine, lest any White Eyes find it and resume mining.

Treasure enthusiast Carl Howe even managed to link Geronimo's treasure to the Lost Dutchman gold of the Superstition Mountains. In the general area was a location known as Geronimo's Cave. In his article, "Did the Dutchman find Montezuma's treasure?" Howe wrote:

> I know personally the story of Geronimo's cave and his supposedly hidden treasure. In the near future, my wife and I together with two other people, are going to examine the cave and its contents. First, of course, it will be necessary for us to obtain the approval of the Apache Council. This may not be easy, as – according to Apache Legend – the cave contains gold and silver that was given to the tribe by their Thunder God. It is also rumored to contain the spoils of many raids upon immigrant wagon trains and homes."[2]

The *El Paso Herald Post* of May 23, 1973, reported on Geronimo's gold and specifically tied it up with the Lost Adams Diggings:

IN HER MEMOIRS published in 1969, Mrs. Fraif Hadlock of El Paso described her efforts to find the gold strike. She said the famed Apache leader Geronimo, while a prisoner at Ft Sill, had admitted killing the prospectors and that Adams had recognized Nana and Geronimo at a reservation as the ones who had killed his companions. The strip of gold—some say 20 miles long—may still be waiting in the malpais. Whether anyone ever got rich from it, it has provided a goldmine of stories to be told over Southwestern campfires for more than a century.

As stated in this chapter's introduction, Geronimo's promise of gold was so vague it could have been located anywhere, but wherever it was, it was certainly somewhere in Apacheria...

Chapter Notes

[1] Lovelace, *Lost Mines and Hidden Treasure*, p.162.
[2] Howe, "Did the Dutchman Find Montezuma's treasure?," *Gold!* (Almanac, 1969), p.61.

COONEY'S BODY IS FOUND

Decomposed Remains of Hardy Old Pioneer Discovered; Met Fate in Wild Blizzard In Mogollons

DISAPPEARED ON OCTOBER 26TH.

Socorro, Feb. 16.—The body of Captain M. Cooney, who went into the Mogollon mountains on a hunting trip late last October, was found yesterday by former Mounted Policeman Bob Lewis. Word reached Socorro this morning of the discovery, ending a search which continued for nearly four months. Cooney left here October 26, drove to Alexander's ranch west of Magdalena, 70 miles, and thence packed into the mountains since which time nothing was heard of him. Captain Cooney, who was looking for a lost mine, was 76 years old.

20.

THE LOST TURNER MINE
MICHAEL COONEY MEETS HIS END

aptain Michael Cooney, brother of Captain James Cooney covered earlier, was among the men that J. Frank Dobie connected to the Lost Adams Diggings in *Apache Gold & Yaqui Silver*. However, the way in which Dobie colored the tale of Cooney didn't present the exact truth. Whether Dobie did this on purpose to enhance his story or by accident is unknown. Dobie's portrait of Cooney was that of an old desert rat and wanderer, constantly on the lookout for the diggings. And while Captain Cooney likely hunted them from time to time, the diggings did not spell his doom as Dobie claimed.

It was in 1883 that Cooney met the man who would eventually cost him his life, albeit inadvertently. His name was Turner, and he asked if Cooney might grubstake him if he went prospecting in the Mogollons for gold. Cooney agreed under the terms that he would share in the findings. Naturally, Turner disappeared never to be seen again—not alive, at least. The next year, Cooney had a chance meeting with Turner's uncle, a former printer from Ohio, in Santa Fe. The man, unaware that his nephew had ever met Cooney, proceeded to tell him that his nephew had written him a letter from Silver City, telling him to come at once as he had found a rich strike along Sycamore creek of gold-tellurium ore of a very high grade. He wrote to his uncle to meet him in Silver City on the Fourth of July of 1883, only Turner never showed.

Michael Cooney as he appeared in an illustrated portrait. James H. Lycons, who met Cooney in the Mogollon Mountains, described him as "a big jolly good-hearted man, a good storyteller, and a genuine opportunist."[1]

Six years later, in 1889, what were presumed to be Turner's remains were found by cowboys working for the T.J. Cattle Company at Sycamore Creek. Around the man's skeleton were eighty-eight spent rounds, implying that he had died fighting the Apache. That same year in the fall, Cooney set out with John Stout and John Foster, a couple of well-weathered mountain men, to search out what was now called the Lost Turner Mine. Cooney would continue this search for years.

As stated before, although Dobie tied Cooney into the Lost Adams Diggings, according to Cooney's friend James H. Lycons, it was really the Lost Turner Mine that led to Cooney's death in the wilderness in 1914. Cooney left on October 26, 1914, promising his wife he would be back in time for Thanksgiving. When he failed to return as promised, his son

Charlie searched the snowy mountains for his father, predicting only to find his remains. And as expected, Cooney's body was found in February of 1915 along Sycamore Creek, where Turner claimed to have found the gold.[2]

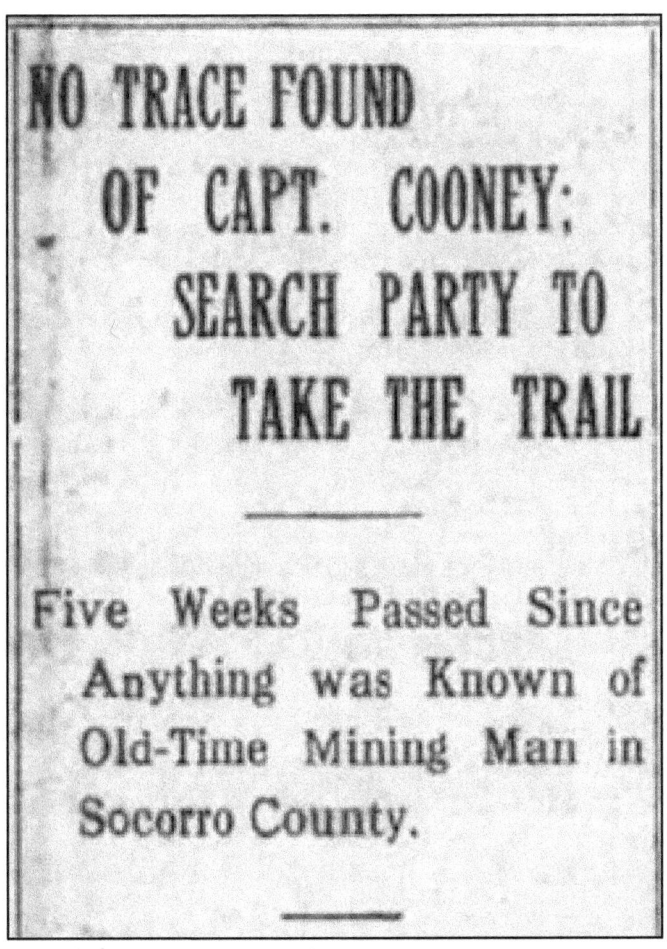

NO TRACE FOUND OF CAPT. COONEY; SEARCH PARTY TO TAKE THE TRAIL

Five Weeks Passed Since Anything was Known of Old-Time Mining Man in Socorro County.

Actually, Cooney's body was found within 100 yards of where Turner himself had been found dead. Since Cooney had specified he wanted to be buried in Socorro and not in the wilderness, the men constructed a stretcher and carried his remains back to civilization. His last journal entry for November 15th read, "It let in a little sunshine today it feels better."

Though Dobie's account of Captain Cooney was at odds with others, it's worth noting that, according to Dobie, gold nuggets valuing $26 were found on Cooney's dead body. If this is true, then perhaps Cooney found at least a trace of the Lost Turner Mine before he died.

Chapter Notes

---

[1] Lycons, "Captain Cooney's Fate," *Old West* (Summer 1970), p.14.

[2] Dobie's account of Turner, who he did not name, was entirely different from other accounts. Dobie had Turner as a "sensitive" young man who the roughneck cowboys delighted in belittling. The young man actually chose to wander the wilderness heading south for Silver City rather than remain at camp. On his trek to Silver City, he stumbled upon a gold ledge within a small canyon. Right or wrong, Dobie decided to connect the canyon to the Lost Adams. From there, the Turner account was basically similar, with the boy returning to Silver City with tales of gold. Eventually he wrote to his uncle, a printer from Kansas City. Odder yet, Dobie made no mention of Cooney having been a former backer who grubstaked Turner in his search. Instead, per Dobie's version, the chance meeting with the uncle in Santa Fe was the first Cooney had ever heard of the young man. Furthermore, Dobie never mentioned Cooney's wife and children in his chapter, leading one to believe he was an aimless prospector who didn't even have a home to return to.

21.

RETURN TO THE LOST ADAMS
THE BALLAD OF JASON BAXTER

Almost as important as Adams himself to the story of the Lost Adams Diggings was a man by the name of Jason Baxter. Brought to light by prospector James McKenna in his beloved book *Black Range Tales*, McKenna met Baxter in the mid-1880s and even accompanied him on a trip to what was probably Sno-Ta-Hay Canyon. Baxter was an ex-soldier who claimed to have found the same canyon as Adams in the mid-1870s. It all started when Baxter heard the collective tales of Adams, Colonel Jacob Snively, and Jake Schaeffer, deducting that all three likely found the same lost canyon of gold. Using the accounts of the three men, Baxter then successfully estimated the general area of the diggings.

As a starting point, Baxter figured the mountain with the woman's face on it, as Schaeffer described it, was likely the Lady of Magdalena. Baxter and a companion, John Adair, set out in the vicinity of the Lady of Magdalena and passed it by on their way to the diggings. Baxter and Adair then came across an even more fantastic landmark that he called Island Mountain. Interestingly, Baxter likened it to the ruins of an ancient civilization, stating that it brought to mind the pyramids of Egypt. Not too far from Island Mountain, Baxter eventually came to the entrance of what looked to be a canyon. Could it be the legendary Lost Adams at last?

As Baxter's luck would have it, his mule actually wandered right through the secret door of Sno-Ta-Hay Canyon. Baxter and Adair followed it inside, seeing many traces of former habitation. Since some signs implied a former Anglo presence, Baxter knew this had to be the canyon discovered by Adams and Schaeffer. "The water increased as we went up and the canyon walls of white quartz became tinted like a rainbow in the evenin' air," Baxter remembered. "All the clays and rocks looked mineralized."[1]

The Lady of Magdalena was a major landmark in Baxter's iteration of the Lost Adams Diggings story.

Baxter and his companion spent the rest of the evening prospecting before finally retiring. However, the next day spelled trouble from the get-go via brewing storm clouds. As it turned out, they foreshadowed something even more dangerous than the looming storm: the Apache guardians of Sno-Ta-Hay Canyon. In a story even more exciting than Adams', amidst a thundering rainstorm that nearly flooded the canyon, Baxter and his companion fled with the Apache hot on their trail. Per McKenna, Baxter related the following:

"We dropped down inside the barricade as a shower of arrows passed over our heads, followed by hellish, blood-curdlin' yells. It was still too dark to see the savages through the eyeholes in our barricade. We waited holdin' our breath, expectin' each moment to be rushed by the red demons. I was lyin' on the left side of the barricade, John bein' in the middle.

"An Apache rose overhead on the cliff throwin' a lance and drawin' fire from Adair. At the same instant eight or ten more of the devils jumped up from their hidin' places just below us and rushed towards the barricade. I pumped my Winchester into them with deadly effect, three of them instantly crumplin' like autumn leaves. Hevin' never before been up against a repeatin' rifle the rest were puzzled and ran back among the boulders. There was a lull in the attack, givin' John time to reload his Sharps.

I warned John to watch out for the Indian above, as the lance had just missed his leg by a hair's breadth. The Apaches did not rush us again. We had them guessin'. We laid inside our barricade all day, and they kept tryin' to reach us from above. About 3 o'clock in the afternoon I sighted an Indian on a nearby cliff givin' signals. As John's rifle had the longer range we traded guns, and they drew on the Indian sentinel topplin' him from the cliff. At the same instant the Indian from above again threw his lance, piercin' John's foot, but John got him, and we had no more trouble from that section. John's foot swelled fast, and we had to cut his shoe to get it off. It sure was hell.

"We could still see the signals and figured they were callin' for help. All day long the black clouds hung above us. We longed for the night to come, for our only hope was in darkness. Our getaway must be made up the canyon, for all the Indians seem to be comin' from below. Night came at last and with it the storm that had held off all day. Lightning flashed, the thunder rolled and cracked as if the mountains were knockin' their heads together. We were in for a night of it and we knew it.[2]

Frontispiece of James A. McKenna in the 1936 first printing of *Black Range Tales*.

The next episode, where the duo escaped in the flooding canyon, was even more exciting:

"John was afraid of a cloudburst at that time of the year. Above the screamin' of the wind and the roarin' of the thunder we could hear the calls of the Indians.

"We made up our minds to risk everything to get away through the storm in the dark. The lightnin' was terrible and dangerous, for the bright flashes might at any minute give us away to the watchin' Indians. We got together a bit of bacon and flour and our water canteens, and made an openin' in our barricade where the shadow laid thickest against the canyon wall. Soon we were creepin' up the canyon, huggin' the wall and tryin' to shrink out of sight and the glarin' lightnin'. The storm raged like a mad bull – such rain as it was, fallin' in sheets and by the bucketful. The canyon soon became a rushin' torrent.

"John had to stop to put on his shoes, and neither of us could ever figure out how he got the shoe over his swollen foot nor how he managed to walk after that, but he did both whisperin' to me between thunderclaps, that we were between the devil and the deep sea and we would sure drown if we didn't get out of that gulch in a hurry. Hardly had he said this when the lightnin' showed us the Mexican mule comin' towards us, still draggin' the lariat rope, probably havin' been driven down by the floodin' waters. He stopped and I caught hold of the rope. John made a halter of it and was soon astraddle. A little farther on we turned into a smaller canyon where the waters were neither so deep nor so swift. The sky became lighter as we went up this gulch which led us finally into quite a valley.

"By the lightnin' flashes we made out an old partly-burned log cabin standin' to one side of the valley. There was no roof and only a few logs were standin'. Close to the ruined cabin we also made out what looked like a sluice box in the pile of lumber; and a short distance away thought we saw two piles of bones. As the Indians, judgin' from their whoops and catcalls, had discovered our escape, we dared not go over to examine the spot. Whippoorwill calls and coyote barks could be heard in all directions except above and to our right.

"The Arroyo soon forked again, we choosin' the one goin' West. We splashed along all night, gettin' to the head of the gulch at daybreak…"[3]

Classic painting of the Apache by Charles Craig c.1903.

From there the two travelers headed towards the Rio Grande in hopes that they might encounter some U.S. Calvary troopers instead of more Apache. Baxter and John Adair made it back to civilization with Adair returning to Pinos Altos. And Baxter, as we all know, eventually drifted onto the homestead of James McKenna where the duo made plans to return to the diggings. What Baxter and McKenna found was quite discouraging, however. When returning to the spot of the canyon, the area appeared to have been decimated in an earthquake.

"From what I see the Lost Diggin's are now in a Lost Canyon, scattered more likely to the head of the Little Colorado River,"[4] Baxter said sadly. "Boys, we sure came to Lost Canyon Diggins," Baxter continued. "There'll never be any yellow nuggets found here unless there comes another earthquake and cloudburst to throw and wash back into the gulch what they took out of it."[5] Baxter then suggested that perhaps next spring they could return and see if the landscape had been altered further in a favorable way instead of a negative one.

After this, Baxter and McKenna began their trek back to civilization. They first stopped at the cabin of the McKenzie family, about thirty miles from Alma. Upon their arrival, there were ominous signs that the two had been followed by either Mexican bandits or Apache. The group proceeded with caution over the course of the next day. McKenna had gone fishing to get dinner for the evening while Baxter remained at the cabin. When McKenna returned, he found signs of an Indian raid along with Baxter's mutilated body.

Vintage stampede illustration.

Shortly after making the grisly discovery, McKenna himself was soon captured by the Apache marauders, but lucky for him, a stampede occurred and he escaped in the chaos.

After the danger had passed, McKenna reflected on how the night before, Baxter had said he knew his time would come when "he found himself camped in a small valley with a stream of water runnin' through it." Baxter claimed that in his vision, a herd of cattle would be grazing along the hillside when suddenly, men, women, and children would begin to run in terror. The men would all have guns in hand, prepared for a fight. "Everyone will run as if the devil were after him," Baxter had said. "When this happens, I'll know my time has come."[6]

And it had.

Chapter Notes

[1] Mckenna, *Black Range Tales*, p.44.
[2] Ibid, p.45.
[3] Ibid, p.46.
[4] Ibid.
[5] Ibid, p.63.
[6] Ibid, p.65.

THE "LOST ADAMS LEAD."

Uncle Sam's Boys After Prospectors on The Navajo Reservation.

ALBUQUERQUE, N. M., March 28.—Great excitement prevails here over the sending of troops into the Navajo reservation after a party of nineteen prospectors who are in the Carriso mountains, about 100 miles north of Gallup. The party has been there for three weeks, and it is alleged have found the "lost Adams diggings." They are well armed and are determined to thoroughly prospect the section or fight. The Indians drove out a party a short time ago that had sunk a thirty foot shaft on a body of very rich native and free gold ore. The large party then went in and the Indians notified the troops at Fort Wingate to take them out. An expedition of seventy-five men left Gallup this morning with rations for a campaign.

The *Montana Helena Independent* of March 29, 1890.

22.

THE LOST ADAMS WAR

NAVAJO GOLD IN THE CARRIZO MOUNTAINS

In early 1890 commenced yet another expedition in search of the Lost Adams Diggings, this one on land encompassed within the Navajo Reservation north of Gallup. As usual, the diggings themselves remained unfound. But, unlike previous excursions, the prospectors did at least find a sizeable quantity of gold—enough that it nearly resulted in the Navajo being removed from their sacred lands.

The first mention of the diggings in 1890 came via the *Forrest City Times* of February 8, which simply and cryptically stated, "The Lost Adams mine is now believed by experts to have been found." That was all the information the paper offered. Whether this blurb was fool's gold or of something more substantial we will likely never know, but exactly a month later a party of men left Gallup for the Carrizo Mountains in search of the Lost Adams.

The *Arizona Weekly Enterprise* of March 29, 1890, reported that the party comprised fifteen men and that they would be met on the way by "one from Socorro of about the same number, when they will make a forced ride through the heart of the Navajo country to the Carrizo mountains." The men were said to have a month's worth of rations plus 5,000 rounds of ammunition. This was, needless to say, a very well-prepared

A letter from a man named R.J. Eilbeck, who had befriended a member of the party of men who had entered the Navajo Reservation "in search of the 'lost Adams' mine" and heard the tale from him, had a letter published in a British paper in 1890. Eilbeck stated in his letter that, "Outside of Adams they were the only white men who ever succeeded in getting into the Navajo reservation and out alive." Eilbeck's account of Adams himself is humorously different from the usual and worth repeating:

> The "lost Adams" mine is named after a man named Adams, who, by some means only known to himself, succeeded in getting into the Carrizo mineral district. He came out only when he required flour, etc., and always brought immense quantities of gold. He was very, very rich, and many attempts were made to track him or follow him, but all such attempts proved unsuccessful. He was finally killed by the Indians, his cabin burned down, and all trace of him wiped out. The mines discovered by the party just in are supposed to be the same as Adams worked.

Lost Adams party. Rather prophetically, the paper ended the piece stating "…if they accomplish what they have set out for, this portion of New Mexico will probably soon experience a mining boom such as the Southwest country never dreamed of."

And indeed, from 1892-1893 there was a mini-gold boom in the Four Corners region, particularly in Utah. However, this mini-gold boom was born more so from media manipulation than it was real gold. For a brief period, newspapers over-exaggerated gold finds in the region and the railroad was more than happy to hop on the bandwagon. Railroad magnates ran ads proclaiming the discoveries, knowing full well that amateur prospectors would begin boarding trains by the hundreds. They did so throughout mid-to-late 1892, but by 1893, very little gold was found, and most of the men had returned home. But, before this, the rumblings out of New Mexico in 1890 certainly helped whet the media's appetite for stories of gold.

And what a sensational tale of adventure it was, with the party of prospectors braving a blazing snowstorm to reach their destination. On Carrizo Mountain they found both the gold they sought and also hostile Navajo. From the moment the men set foot in the mountains, they were reportedly besieged by a group led by Chief Black Horse, who threatened to kill the men if they didn't leave. The prospectors guarded their camp day and night from potential attacks, and seeing this, Black Horse tried to recruit the neighboring Ute tribe in his efforts to rid his land of the prospectors. For their troubles, the Utes could split the spoils of the assault, those being the prospector's supplies and livestock. For reasons unknown, the Utes didn't care to participate.

Bilii Lizhini, aka Black Horse, and Taiyoni, aka Squeezer, c.1904.
(Photograph by Sim Schwemberger)

A prospector and his burro ascending a mountain c. 1900.

Instead, the Navajo would seek aid from the soldiers at forts Defiance and Wingate, both of which oversaw the Navajo Reservation. Reports of the soldiers setting out to arrest the men were quickly sensationalized, with numerous papers across the country picking up on the story of a group of prospectors illegally mining "the Lost Adams Diggings" on the Navajo Reservation.

One of the more sensational blurbs ran the headline "GOLD OR BLOOD" in the *Winona Daily Republican* of March 29, 1890:

> Great excitement prevails here over the sending of troops into the Navajo reservation after a party of nineteen prospectors who are in the Carriso mountains about one hundred miles north of Gallup. The party have been there three weeks and it is alleged have found "Lost Adams Diggings." They are well armed and determined to thoroughly prospect the section or fight.

A lengthier variation of that article reported that the prospectors had "sunk a thirty-foot shaft on a body of very rich native and free gold ore." It continued that the Navajo went to the troops of Fort Wingate for aid to "take them out."

Tradition has woven a web of mystery and a glamor of romance around the Chuzco and Carrizo mountains. As far back as '69 parties from California attempted to invade and explore the Carrizos, whose fabulous wealth has been measured only by the anxious miner. The Adams party left a legend that three days' travel from Wingate with pack animals they found gold for all and graves for most of their party upon the Navajo reservation. Again, by a party from California consisting of twenty-seven men, only two of whom escaped to put the fact upon record that gold and death are inseparable companions in the Carrizo mountains.—San Juan Times.

This short blurb from the *Santa Fe New Mexican* of July 31, 1891, was yet another source that alluded to the idea that the Carrizo Mountain gold was the source of the Lost Adams Diggings.

"LOST ADAMS DIGGINGS."

The Mountain of Gold Found by a Party of Miners in New Mexico.

ALBUQUERQUE, N. M., March 29.—Great excitement prevails here over sending of troops into the Navajo Reservation after a party of nineteen prospectors who are in the Carriso Mountains about 100 miles north of Gallup. The party has been there three weeks, and, it is alleged, have found "Lost Adams Diggings." They are well armed, and are determined to thoroughly prospect the section. The Indians moved out a party, a short time ago, that had sunk a thirty foot shaft on a body of very rich native and free gold ore. The large party then went in and the Indians notified troops at Fort Wingate to take them out. An expedition of 75 men left Gallup yesterday with 30,-000 pounds of rations for the campaign.

From the *Kaukauna Sun* of April 4, 1890.

GOLD OR BLOOD.

A PARTY OF PROSPECTORS PURSUED BY TROOPS.

ALBUQUERQUE. N. M., March 29.— Great excitement prevails here over the sending of troops into the Nevajo reservation after a party of nineteen prospectors who are in the Carriso' mountains about one hundred miles north of Gallup. The party have been there three weeks and it is alleged have found "Lost Adams Diggings." They are well armed and determined to thoroughly prospect the section or fight.

From the *Winona Daily Republican* of March 29, 1890.

Navajo nugget from Gallup: A company called the Carrizo Mountain Mining Co., W. A. Smith, president, and Ed. R. Somers, secretary, with principal office at Gallup, N. M., has been organized here for the purpose of owning and operating gold and silver mines in the Carrizo mountains, Patterson mining district, Apache county, A. T.

This brief blurb from the *Santa Fe New Mexican* of April 18, 1890, demonstrated the excitement generated over the gold reports.

Apacheria Gold

According to most reports, 75 soldiers left Fort Wingate with 30,000 pounds of rations for the journey. The soldiers arrived on the 20th day and arrested the men peaceably, as reports said no men were harmed or put up any resistance. The men were allowed to take their gold with them, and some of it was sent to Washington, D.C. One paper reported:

> The company will send specimens of the wonderfully rich ore to Washington and try to secure the passage of a bill segregating a district 20 miles square from the Navajo reservation as a mineral district.[1]

Over the next two years, several efforts to make this come to pass were undertaken. An article published in the *Boston Daily Globe* of May 13, 1890, stated, "L. S. Gordon of Wingate. N. M., is in this city endeavoring to organize a company to open the Navajo reservation in New Mexico for the reason that he has a certain clue to the famous lost Adams mine."

The article "Navajo Gold Fields," published in the *Santa Fe Weekly Sun* of November 29, 1890, quoted the Navajo agent of the time as stating, "There is gold enough there to make us all rich, and soon as the Indian title can be extinguished, or the country can be in any way opened to the operations of prospectors and miners you will hear of developments that will astonish the country." The plan was to give the Navajo new lands whilst opening the Carrizos to the public.[2] There was even talk of building a new road from Gallup to the mountains for this purpose.

The *Arizona Republic* of January 19, 1891, reported that,

> Major C. E. Vandever, late agent for the Navajos, is in town this week and states that the accounts that have appeared from time to time in this journal of the richness of the gold fields in the Carrizo mountains are not at all exaggerated. On the other hand, he says, the whole truth has not been told, and he believes the district to be much richer in the abundance of the precious metals which it contains than the most extravagant accounts have ever represented it to be.

INDIANS TURBULENT.

The Navajoes Reported to be Preparing to Go On the Warpath.

COLORADO SPRINGS, COLO., Jan. 19. —Advices received by T. J. Matthews, of Colorado City, from his partner, T. E. Lacone, of Cortez, Colo, state that the Navajo Indians in that vicinity are arranging for war. The Indians claim the Carizo Mountains as a part of their reservation, although recent Government surveys locate the line further up the San Juan. Rich gold fields abound in the mountains, which have been known to Lacone and others for some time. The Indians have molded golden bullets and exhibited them, but they vow the death of any white miners who invade their reservation. Since the survey was made Lacone and other miners have staked claims and are now camped upon them. They are prepared to defend their rights. Meanwhile the Indians have retired to their reservation, and an uprising is feared, which, however, may not occur till in the spring. The camp is thirty miles from Cortez.

Hazel Green Herald of February 3, 1893.

Vandever stated that he received a letter from the Commissioner of Indian Affairs requesting that he, as the Secretary of the Interior, open the lands for mining. In the typical palavering of the day, it was even argued that this would no doubt protect the Navajo from a deluge of potentially dangerous prospectors. In other words, the government would get the gold and boot the Navajo off for their own good. This naturally greatly upset the Navajo Nation, as the lands were sacred.

THE EXPEDITION LEAVING FORT WINGATE.
[*Photographed for the "Examiner."*]

Illustration from the *San Francisco Examiner* of May 1, 1892.

In May of 1892, a government-sanctioned expedition under the command of General McCook, including two geologists and three professional prospectors, was about to commence from Fort Wingate to explore the Carrizo Mountains. The *San Francisco Examiner* of May 1, 1892, stated, "This is not like the hundreds of expeditions that have started on the same errand and been turned back by the Indians. This one starts under Government auspices, with a general of the United States army in command, under the escort of a troop of cavalry."[3]

General McCook and his men arrived in the mountains on May 18, and on the evening of the 20th, Chief Black Horse came to their camp and entered into council with the General from that day until the 24th. Chief Black Horse explained that the mountains were "a place of worship" for the Navajo and that the tribe did not wish to part from them.

More than anything, the Navajo feared that mining of the Carrizo Mountains would result in the desecration of Shiprock Peak, shown above, which was sacred to the tribe. A particularly interesting legend claimed that during the Spanish occupation of what is today New Mexico, the Spanish priests forced the Navajo to work a mine near Shiprock. After many Navajo had died due to harsh labor, according to legend, the Thunder God became angry and sent a great deluge, causing the mine to cave in between two mountains. After this, according to the myth as it was regurgitated in the *San Francisco Examiner* of May 1, 1892, an undead army was raised to drive away the Spanish conquistadors that didn't perish in the flood:

> Then all the Navajos who had been killed in fighting the invaders were awakened from death by the shaking, so fierce it was, and they fell upon the armored soldiers and drove them into a canyon, from which they could not escape, and rolled down bowlders on them until they were all dead and buried. Ever since that time the Navajos have been in possession of the Ship Rock peak.

Reports stated that McCook's expedition found and retrieved gold on May 26th, and on May 30th, five sacks of gold ore passed through Gallup to be taken back to Fort Wingate, and from there, it shipped to Washington. News of the find spread, and the *Gallup Gleaner*, per the *Silver Belt*, reported that camps of "sooners" could be seen setting up along the banks of the San Juan River "waiting for the opening of the new El Dorado."

Group of Fort Wingate surveyors in the 1880s.

As stated earlier, the entire Four Corners region was fired up over gold during the time, and so papers were more than happy to exaggerate any gold talk. However, as was the case of the "mini-gold boom" to overtake Utah that same year, there was actually little gold to be found on the Navajo Reservation. Contrary to newspaper claims of the time, an official document from the Arizona Geological Survey by William L. Chenoweth, "The Carrizo 'gold' mine" (1989), told another story:

> During two weeks in the mountains [the McCook party] found small amounts of copper and iron pyrite, but no gold, silver or lead deposits. Eighteen of the most promising samples were assayed; three samples averaged 2.95 ounces of silver and 0.015 and 0.025 ounces of gold per ton. The commission of Indian Affairs then issued a report stating "that the region was barren of metallic wealth and worthless for mining purposes".[4]

This certainly proved fortunate for the Navajo and the matter was dropped. Though the Lost Adams may be fool's gold for some, the search for the diggings nearly had devastating consequences for the Navajo and their sacred lands.[5]

Chapter Notes

---

[1] Actually, the expedition led to more than just discoveries of gold and silver, but also of coal and petroleum.

[2] A similar, less publicized incident preceded this in 1875, when the acting Indian Agent identified only as Arny, wanted to open the Carrizos for mining of gold.

[3] *San Francisco Examiner* (May 1, 1892).

[4] Chenoweth, "The Carrizo 'gold' mine," Arizona Geological Survey Contributed Report (1989) CR-89-B.

[5] There was a flare up of threats to mine the Navajo Nation land again in 1896, though these reports rarely, if ever mentioned gold, and seemed to be more interested in other minerals like copper. See Appendix III for more.

APPENDIX I

Many intriguing articles relating to the discovery of gold on the Navajo lands in 1890 were published, and in the following Appendices, a few of them will be reprinted in full. The first comes from the Florence Arizona Weekly Enterprise *of April 19, 1890.*

"CALLED BACK"
The prospectors are sent home by the soldiers –
the goal is there and the gold is there
(Gallup Elk)

The prospecting party that left here on March 10 for the Carrizo mountain, where glittering wealth was reported to be in store for those who dared to run the Navajo gauntlet to seek the precious metals, have returned to Gallup, dirty, fat and glad.

It must be remembered that this mountain of wealth has been strictly guarded by the Navajo tribe for many years, and the white man who dared to penetrate the secret treasure vaults of this generous mountain of wealth, took his life in his hand and considered him so fortunate if he could once more reach the "home base" and tell of what he saw.

Many a poor prospector has been lured to death by the wonderful tales of wealth encased in this mountain. Many went, saw, but couldn't conquer, and very few got back to friends to tell of their disappointment.

It has been generally believed that in this mountain range was located the "lost Adams diggings," but the mystery that surrounded this sacred (to the Navajos) mountain was never solved until the brave and determined pioneer boys that composed this hazardous expedition penetrated the heart of the Navajo country and lifted the veil from the golden wealth that has been so long hidden from the greedy eyes of the avaricious white man and which has been so closely guarded by his red brother.

As soon as opportunity permitted a reporter waited on the boys and elicited the fact that the trip out was made with little or no opposition; in fact, they made a "sneak" on the Indians by running into the mountain at night, and were fortified and prepared to receive any number of hostiles that Black Horse, the war chief, might muster.

According to expectation, Black Horse was on the ground soon after, with a poorly organized war party. His threats were many and of a character to shatter the nerves of the bravest. Our boys were equal to the occasion, however and told his redskinship what they were there for, what they intended to do, and that if he was hankering after capillary ornaments for his hogan to get his measly braves in shape and they would entertain them to the extent of over 5000 rounds of Winchester capsules.

The boys said the old duffer pleaded, begged and threatened, but his hostile demonstrations amounted to naught. After sizing up the exterminating propensities of the prospectors Dark Horse reluctantly made a sorrowful retreat, but immediately sent couriers to the agency, Fort Defiance, and to Fort Wingate, for assistance in having the prospectors removed. He also went over to the Ute reservation and tried to induce the Utes to assist him in making war on the whites, offering as an inducement one half the guns and forces captured.

In the meantime, the boys were hustling to find the "precious." Snow covered the ground everywhere, but croppings of mineral liberally covered the mountain.

They were on the mountain only three or four days when the soldiers that were sent out from Fort Wingate brought them out. However, they succeeded in making a number of locations and they brought back with them some of the finest specimens of silver and gold bearing quartz we ever saw.

The boys are elated over the prospects, yet they are not satisfied, as they believe there are millions of naked wealth undiscovered lying there for those who have the nerve to go after it.

Apacheria Gold

This article is not colored. We have endeavored to give the simple facts without any boom foolishness.

Though the article had a haughty, condescending tone, history and the Navajo got the last laugh.

APPENDIX II

The New York Sun *of November 24, 1890, reported that the find was "in the Navajo reservation that the 'First Adams Diggings' are supposed to be located." In that issue was published a letter from one of the miners that stated,*

"On the 11th of March last, a party of eighteen of us started from Gallup on a prospecting trip to the Carrizo Mountains, on the Navajo reservation. We ascended the mountain on the 17th of March, the elevation being about 2,600 feet; very little timber, grass, or water. On the 10th a chief—Black Horse-of the Navajos attempted to drive us off. The formation at the foot of the mountain and nearly all the way up was sandstone. We found some granite. And in three days we struck a quartzite lode carrying gold. The Indians bothered us considerably, and in the mean time, a snow storm coming on, we retired down the mountain. Three of our men left us. We found the snow four or five feet deep in the canyons. The distance from Gallup was 125 miles. We then went north about twenty-five miles to Nolan's trading post, on the San Juan River, for supplies. There we found that the Navajos had offered the Utes half of our horses and arms to assist in driving us off. We went south around the west side of the mountain and ascended it again. We only had five prospectors in the party, and had to guard our camp and horses. However, we discovered seven different quartz leads, carrying free gold. One lead is sixty feet wide, and shows for nearly two miles. An assay cropping taken from this lead went $425 per ton. The other leads vary from $350 to $375 per ton.

"It was on account of rock taken from this lead that the Indians killed Capt. Swift two years ago.[1] We made eighty locations, and the Indians, then finding they could not drive us out, got two troops of cavalry, who arrested us and took us to Defiance, and put us off the reservation. We also discovered both coal and iron veins. To reach Carrizo Mountain it is necessary to go by rail from Albuquerque to Gallup, and then by pack animals or wagons through the Navajo country, or east of the reservation and down the north side, entering from Colorado."

Section Notes

---

[1] This was the man killed in R.C. Patterson's 1888 expedition.

APPENDIX III

There was an addendum of sorts to the saga of the Navajo gold in the form of an 1896 episode, where talks resumed of mining the Navajo lands. The following blurb was published in the Vermont Watchman and State Journal *of May 20, 1896:*

Chief Blackhorse of the Navajo Indian tribe and a powerful element of the tribe are opposing the invasion of the Carrizo mountain gold field in New Mexico. Trouble is likely to ensue if they undertake to mine in that region. A company of United States soldiers has been ordered to the vicinity of Farlington [sic; Farmington], and all citizens entering the Navajo reservation are requested to secure passports from the agent under penalty of arrest and confiscation of their effects.

The Santa Fe New Mexican *of May 12, 1896, reported:*

TROUBLE BREWING

Some months ago the New Mexican made mention of the fact that a syndicate headed by Mr. John H. P. Voorhees, of Denver, a nephew of Senator Voorhees, of Indiana, sought of both the government and the Indians the privilege to prospect and mine for the precious metals supposed to exist in the Carrizo mountains on the Navajo reservation.

For many years fabulous stories have been rife of immense natural treasures hidden in these mountains and many efforts have been made to prospect for the same. But the Navajoes have jealously guarded these mountains against white prospectors, and, supported by the strong arm of the government, have so far succeeded in driving off alleged trespassers and preventing even the more venturesome from gaining more than just enough information to excite additional cupidity and curiosity in their minds. But it seems that Voorhees and his associates, by the liberal use of bribes and many glittering promises of larger ones in the future, succeeding in persuading a large section of the Navajo tribe to grant them the exclusive right to prospect and mine for gold and silver in the Carrizo mountains. This arrangement, however, did not meet the approbation of another section of the tribe headed by the noted and intrepid Black Horse, war chief of the tribe, and these Indians have exercised all their power and influence to destroy the same. But this opposition proved unavailing. The will of the majority prevailed, and, evidently with the sanction of the Indian bureau, the syndicate will very soon begin the contemplated work.

This causes trouble from two sources— the dissatisfied and dangerous minority of the Navajoes under Black Horse and the many miners outside of the privileged syndicate who are determined to share in the prospective benefits of prospecting the Carrizo mountains. If this happens, says the San Juan Times, that United States troops have been ordered from Fort Wingate to guard the mountains named from all other prospectors than those who have the special permission noted, and that persons crossing the soil of the sacred Navajo reservation on ordinary business errands, such as going from Farmington to Gallup or Wingate, are required to protect themselves from arrest or violence by procuring passports from the Navajo Indian agent. Sensational news from the Carrizo mountains may be looked for any day.

The Santa Fe New Mexican *of June 13, 1896, followed up with this report which would seem to allude to New Mexico's nefarious Santa Fe Ring:*

The excitement over the leasing of the Carrizo mountains for mining purposes is increasing. It is just possible that trouble may occur. It seems strange that these few men could have gained permission to open the mines. What is the reason? First has McCook practiced deception in the matter, and is McCook now probably in the syndicate? Is this a mere bubble of a syndicate of big men who use congressional and governmental influence to start and run a side mining concern? Are these men taking advantage of the wonderful stories of these hills

173

spread abroad everywhere, of the legends of the Navajos so well known, to excite public imagination and so secure a big thing by selling stock in this concern? We shall know more about this soon, and it is a matter that the public should inform themselves upon.—San Juan Times.

From there, talk of mining the Navajo Nation due to the Carrizo Mountain gold dropped off and did not resume from what I can find.

BIBLIOGRAPHY

Books

Ball, Eve with Nora Henn and Lynda A. Sanchez. *Indeh: An Apache Odyssey*. University of Oklahoma Press, 1988 (second edition).

Childress, David Hatcher. *Lost Cities and Ancient Mysteries of the Southwest*. Adventures Unlimited Press, 2009.

Conrotto, Eugene L. *Lost Gold and Silver Mines of the Southwest*. Dover, 1963/1991.

Cremony, John C. *Life Among the Apache*. A. Roman & Company, 1868.

Dobie, J. Frank. *Apache Gold & Yaqui Silver*. Little, Brown and Company, 1939.

French, Richard. *Four Days From Fort Wingate: The Lost Adams Diggings*. Caxton Printers, Ltd., 1994.

------------- *Return to the Lost Adams Diggings*. Kindle Edition.

Jameson, W.C. *Lost Mines and Buried Treasures of Arizona*. University of New Mexico Press, 2009.

Jones, Fayette Alexander. *New Mexico Mines and Minerals*. Sylvanite Publishing, 2015 reprint (originally published 1904).

Julyan, Robert. *The Place Names of New Mexico: Revised Edition*. University of New Mexico Press, 1998.

Kutz, Jack. *Mysteries and Miracles of New Mexico*. Rhombus Press, 1988.

Lovelace, Leland. *Lost Mines and Hidden Treasure*. The Naylor Company, 1956.

McKenna, James A. *Black Range Tales*. The Rio Grande Press, 1936/1984.

Mitchell, John D. *Lost Mines of the Great Southwest*. The Rio Grande Press, Inc., 1933/1970.

Penfield, Thomas. *Dig Here! Lost Mines & Buried Treasure of the Southwest*. Adventures Unlimited Press, 1962/2004.

Purcell, Jack. *The Lost Adams Diggings: Myth, Mystery and Madness*. Nine Lives Press, 2003.

Robinson, Sherry. *Apache Voices: Their Stories of Survival as Told to Eve Ball*. University of New Mexico Press, 2000.

Simmons, Marc. *Treasure Trails of the Southwest*. University of New Mexico Press, 1994.

Stanley, F. *The Magdalena (New Mexico) Story*. By the author, 1973.

Sweeney, Edwin R. *Mangas Coloradas: Chief of the Chiricahua Apaches*. University of Oklahoma Press, 2011.

Thrapp, Dan. *Juh: An Incredible Indian*. Texas Western Press, 1992.

Articles

Bandelier, Adolph. "'Montezuma' of the Pueblo Indians." *American Anthropologist* (Vol.5. October 1892).

Carson, Kit. "The Shadow of Magdalena." *Frontier Times* (Aug/Sep 1963).

Chenoweth, William L. "The Carrizo 'gold' mine." Arizona Geological Survey Contributed Report (1989) CR-89-B.

Connell, Charles T. "Golden Bullets." *Arizona Republic* (April 18, 1928).

Everleth, Robert W. "Our Lady on the Mountain—history, folklore, and geology of Magdalena Peak." *New Mexico Geology* (2006).

Galbraith, Den. "Iron Door Mine of Blue Canyon." *Frontier Times* (Sep/Oct 1964).

Harden, Paul. "Buried Treasure." *El Defensor Chieftain* (March 2012).

Howe, Carl. "Did the Dutchman find Montezuma's Treasure?" *Gold!* (Almanac, 1969).

Jenkinson, Michael. "Bonanza in the Mogollons." *Frontier Times* (September 1971).

Lycons, James H. "Captain Cooney's Fate." *Old West* (Summer 1970).

Mason, Frank. "The Mountain That Disappeared." *Frontier Times* (June/July 1963).

Matson, Frederick. "Arizona's Lost Canyon of Gold." *Real West* (May 1965).

Phillips, Jerry. "A Pilot's Opinion of the Lost Adams." *Gold!* (Fall 1975).

Rusell, W.C. "An Indian Gave Masonic Distress Sign." *Frontier Times* (October 1924).

INDEX

ABOUT THE AUTHOR

John LeMay was born and raised in Roswell, NM, the "UFO Capital of the World." He is the author of over 50 books, many of them on the history of the Southwest such as *Tall Tales and Half Truths of Billy the Kid*, and *Roswell USA: Towns That Celebrate UFOs, Lake Monsters, Bigfoot and Other Weirdness*. In addition to non-fiction, he is also the author of the novels *The Noted Desperado Pancho Dumez* and *Once Upon a Time in Fort Sumner*. He is also the editor/publisher of *Strange West Magazine* and has written for Western journals and magazines such as *True West*, *The Coalition Journal*, the *Tombstone Epitaph*, and the *Wild West History Association Journal*. He is a Past President of the Board of Directors for the Historical Society for Southeast New Mexico.

The following titles are available for purchase on Amazon.com, and are available to bookstores at a wholesale discount via Ingram Content Group (ISBNs of available editions listed for this purpose)

CRYPTOZOOLOGY/COWBOYS & SAURIANS

Cowboys & Saurians: Prehistoric Beasts as Seen by the Pioneers explores dinosaur sightings from the pioneer period via real newspaper reports from the time. Well-known cases like the Tombstone Thunderbird are covered along with more obscure cases like the Crosswicks Monster and more. Softcover (357 pp/5.06" X 7.8") Suggested Retail: $19.95 ISBN: 978-1-7341546-1-0

Cowboys & Saurians: Ice Age zeroes in on snowbound saurians like the Cerato-saurus of the Arctic Circle and a Tyrannosaurus of the Tundra, as well as sightings of Ice Age megafauna like mammoths, glyptodonts, Sarkastodons and Saber-toothed tigers. Tales of a land that time forgot in the Arctic are also covered. Softcover (264 pp/5.06" X 7.8") Suggested Retail: $14.99 ISBN: 978-1-7341546-7-2

Southerners & Saurians takes the series formula of exploring newspaper accounts of monsters in the pioneer period with an eye to the Old South. In addition to dinosaurs are covered Lizardmen, Frogmen, giant leeches and mosquitoes, and the Dingocroc, which might be an alien rather than a prehistoric survivor. Softcover (202 pp/5.06" X 7.8") Suggested Retail: $13.99 ISBN: 978-1-7344730-4-9

Cowboys & Saurians South of the Border explores the saurians of Central and South America, like the Patagonian Plesiosaurus that was really an lemisch, plus tales of the Neo-Mylodon, a menacing monster from underground called the Minhocao, Glyptodonts, and even Bolivia's three-headed dinosaur! Softcover (412 pp/ 5.06"X7.8") Suggested Retail: $17.95 ISBN: 978-1-953221-73-5

UFOLOGY/THE REAL COWBOYS & ALIENS IN CONJUNCTION WITH ROSWELL BOOKS

The Real Cowboys and Aliens: Early American UFOs explores UFO sightings in the USA between the years 1800-1864. Stories of encounters sometimes involved famous figures in U.S. history such as Lewis and Clark, and Thomas Jefferson.Hardcover (242pp/6" X 9") Softcover (262 pp/5.06" X 7.8") Suggested Retail: $24.99 (hc)/$15.95(sc) ISBN: 978-1-7341546-8-9\(hc)/978-1-7344 730-8-7(sc)

The second entry in the series, *Old West UFOs*, covers reports spanning the years 1865-1895. Includes tales of Men in Black, Reptilians, Spring-Heeled Jack, Sasquatch from space, and other alien beings, in addition to the UFOs and airships. Hardcover (276 pp/6" X 9") Softcover (308 pp/5.06" X 7.8") Suggested Retail: $29.95 (hc)/$17.95(sc) ISBN: 978-1-7344730-0-1 (hc)/ 978-1-73447 30-2-5 (sc)

The third entry in the series, *The Coming of the Airships,* encompasses a short time frame with an incredibly high concentration of airship sightings between 1896-1899. The famous Aurora, Texas, UFO crash of 1897 is covered in depth along with many others. Hardcover (196 pp/6" X 9") Softcover (222 pp/5.06" X 7.8") Suggested Retail: $24.99 (hc)/$15.95(sc) ISBN: 978-1-7347816 -1-8 (hc)/978-1-7347816-0-1(sc)

Featuring cases the authors missed, *The Lost Cases* covers things such as the skyquakes recorded by Lewis and Clark, airships and the Spanish American War, Pancho Villa and crystal skulls, lost alien tribe of the Tundra, invisible alien monsters, the Great Moon Hoax of 1835, hellhounds and airships, the Sonora Airship Club and more. Softcover (252 pp/5.06" X 7.8") Suggested Retail: $18.99 ISBN: 978-1-953221-55-1

Cowboys & Saurians: Dinosaurs Down Under takes the series to Australia to explore tales of the cattle devouring Burrunjor, the dreaded Diprotodon, the terrible Tantanoola Tiger, the marsupial Sasquatch known as the Yowie, plus Thylacines, Bunyips, giant rabbits, Megalodons and dinosaurs in nearby New Zealand. Softcover (240 pp/ 5.06" X 7.8") Suggested Retail: $14.95 ISBN: 978-1-953221-34-6

As the title suggest, *Cowboys & Saurians in the Modern Era* takes the series into the 20th Century with tales of the Texas Pterosaur flap of 1976, the Bladenboro Beast of the 1950s, the Busco Turtle Beast of the 1940s, dinosaur sightings in the Great Depression and far out tales of mini-mastodons, dinosaur men, and Snallygasters. Softcover (320 pp/ 5.06" X 7.8") Suggested Retail: $19.95 ISBN: 978-1-953221-22-3

Settlers & Serpents wrangles the best "Snaik Stories" of the Southwest and beyond in a single volume. Whether it's simple giant snakes or lake serpents, they're corralled in the pages within. Also included are entries on the Leviathan in Mesoamerica and the Southwest plus a detailed look at the giant rattlesnake of Pecos Pueblo. Softcover (180 pp/ 5.06" X 7.8") Suggested Retail: $14.99 ISBN: 978-1-953221-21-6

Written for young readers ages 9-12, *Monsters of the Old South* collects the best creature stories of White River Monster, Green Eyes, the Crocodingo, the Averasboro Gallinipper, the Tennessee Snake Woman, the Arkansas Gowrow, Bigfoot in the Mississippi River and more. Softcover (122 pp/4.25" X 7") Suggested Retail: $12.99 ISBN: 978-17347816-9-4

Early 20th Century UFOs kicks off a new series that investigates UFO sightings of the early 1900s. Includes tales of UFOs sighted over the *Titanic* as it sunk, Nikola Tesla receiving messages from the stars, an alien being found encased in ice, and a possible virus from outer space!Hardcover (196 pp/6" X 9") Softcover (222 pp/5.06" X 7.8") Suggested Retail: $27.99 (hc)/$16.95(sc) ISBN: 978-1-7347816-1-8 (hc)/978-1-73478 16-0-1(sc)

UFOs in the Roaring Twenties takes a look at UFO sightings in the 1920s just as the title suggests, along with accounts of Mothman in Nebraska, Lincoln LaPaz's first UFO case, Men in Black investigating an airship crash in Braxton County, West Virginia, Camden's Cosmic Sniper, and much more! Softcover (248 pp/5.06" X 7.8") Suggested Retail: $19.99 ISBN: 978-1-953221-51-3

UFOs of the Turbulent Thirties concludes the authors' investigation of the last unexplored decade of Ufology in the Great Depression with accounts of Mothman, Ghost Fliers, Nazi Bells, the Underground City of the Lizard People, a vanished village on the tundra, and even gangsters and aliens. Softcover (212 pp/5.06" X 7.8") Suggested Retail: $17.95 ISBN: 978-1-953221-35-3

Written for young readers ages 9-12, *Space Monsters of the Old West* collects the best alien sightings of the Wild West including Mummies from Mars, Bigfoot from the Moon, Pascagoula's space ghouls, the Crawfordsville Monster, Spring-Heeled Jack, Blobs from space, and even the dinosaurian alien creatures that invaded Van Meter, Iowa. Softcover (120 pp/4.25" X 7") Suggested Retail: $12.99 ISBN: 978-1-953221-87-2

Cowboys & Monsters features potentially true stories of real vampires, werewolves, and even mummies unique to America's Wild West period. Examples include the cursed mummy of John Wilkes Booth, New Orleans immortal vampire Jacques St. Germain, precursors to the Beast of Bray Road, and the origins of Skinwalker Ranch. Softcover (316 pp/5.06" X 7.8") Suggested Retail: $19.99 ISBN: 978-1-953221-46-9

The first entry in this trilogy of non-fiction terror sinks its teeth into the lore of the vampire in North America and Mexico, with detailed rundowns on the vampire hunters of Exeter, Rhode Island, a tribe of Bat People, the nocturnal shape-shifting vampire witches of Tlaxcala, and the immortal ways of Comte St. Germain in New Orleans and more. Softcover (200 pp/ 5.06" X 7.8") Suggested Retail: $12.99 ISBN: 978-1-953221-38-4

Mummies of the Americas explores Death Valley's city of the Dead, King Tut's Tomb along the Arkansas, the Egyptian City of the Grand Canyon plus the famous mummies of John Wilkes Boothe, Elmer McCurdy, the Cardiff Giant, the Mummy of Helldorado, and even Billy the Kid's pickled trigger finger! Softcover (200 pp/5.06" X 7.8") Suggested Retail: $12.99 ISBN: 978-1-953221-37-7

Cowboys & Dogmen is devoted to tales of werewolves of the Wild West including the dreaded Navajo skinwalker, the Watrous Werewolf, the Beast of the Land Between Lakes, the Hellhounds of El Dorado Canyon, the dreaded Dog Eater, the Wahhoo, the Wolf Man of Versailles, the Michigan Dog-Man and more! Softcover (212 pp/5.06" X 7.8") Suggested Retail: $12.99 ISBN: 978-1-953221-36-0

The first novel from historian John LeMay weaves a fantastic web of fiction via real life mysteries and legends of New Mexico, namely the puzzling theft and return of Billy the Kid's tombstone in 1976, the legend of the Lost Adams Diggings, the villainous Santa Fe Ring, and the enigmatic Acoma Mesa. Softcover (250 pp/5.5" X 7.5") Suggested Retail: $14.95 ISBN: 978-1-953221-42-1

The year is 1950, and old timers connected to the long-dead outlaw Billy the Kid are turning up murdered in New Mexico. Some blame the killings on the avenging witch of the Navajo nation, the skinwalker, while others think it's no coincidence that a man claiming to be a surviving Billy the Kid is set to meet with the governor soon... Softcover (260 pp/5.5" X 7.5") Suggested Retail: $16.95 ISBN: 978-1-953221-32-2

Roswell, USA, the long-forgotten debut work of John LeMay, is available again and covers the minutia of the infamous Roswell UFO Crash of 1947. Notable chapters include tales of an alien ghost haunting the old airbase, monsters in the nearby Bottomless Lakes, and even a dinosaur sighting outside of town. Softcover (248 pp/6" X 9") Suggested Retail: $14.95 ISBN: 978-0-9817597-5-3

This biography, for the first time ever, tells the history of western journalist Ash Upson, who ghostwrote Pat Garrett's *The Authentic Life of Billy the Kid* in 1882 and also reproduces many of Upson's letters that detailed the harsh realities of frontier life in New Mexico during the turbulent Lincoln County War. Softcover (318 pp/5.5" X 8.5") Suggested Retail: $16.99 ISBN: 978-1953221919

www.ingramcontent.com/pod-product-compliance
Lightning Source LLC
Chambersburg PA
CBHW071354120626
46546CB00002B/682